Amazing
NEW ZEALAND

Chris Chittenden

REED

Published by Reed Children's Books, an imprint of Reed Publishing (NZ) Ltd, 39 Rawene Road, Birkenhead, Auckland. Associated companies, branches and representatives throughout the world.

This book is copyright. Except for the purposes of fair reviewing, no part of this publication may be reproduced or transmitted in any form or by any means, electronic or mechanical, including photocopying, recording, or any information storage and retrieval system, without permission in writing from the publisher.
Infringers of copyright render themselves liable to prosecution.

Text © 2000 Chris Chittenden
The author asserts his moral rights in this work.

© Ian Baker, photographs pp 16 (top), 18 (top), 44 (bottom), 45 (middle), 72 (top)
© Charles Cooper, photographs pp 19 (left and bottom right), 28 (top), 36 (bottom), 74 (bottom)
© Peter Janssen, photographs pp 22 (bottom), 24 (bottom), 27 (top left), 32 (top)
© Vicki Marsdon, photograph p 37 (bottom right)
© Geoff Moon, photographs pp 63 (middle right), 74 (top), 75 (bottom left and right)
© Anne Mortimer, photograph p 68 (bottom)
© Stephen Robinson, photographs pp 23 (top), 34 (bottom left and right), 56 (bottom right)
© Holger Leue, all remaining photographs

First published 2000
ISBN 1 86948 866 0

Printed in New Zealand

To Margaret, Jaya and Tim

For letting me indulge in what I love doing —
exploring and sharing New Zealand's unique natural
and cultural environments.

contents

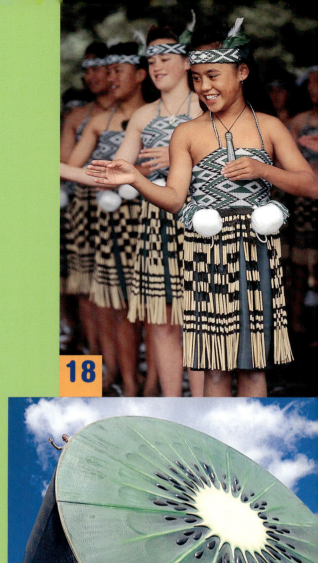

New Zealand overviews and maps		6
Northland	– Birthplace of a Nation	10
	– The Winterless North	12
Auckland	– City of Sails	14
	– City of Volcanoes	16
	– Pacific City	18
Coromandel	– Heart of Gold	20
Waikato	– From Cowbells to Caverns	22
	– A Powerful River	24
Bay of Plenty	– Kiwifruit Country	26
East Cape	– First to See the Sun	28

18

26

42

Hawke's Bay	– Fragile Fruitbowl	30
Volcanic Plateau	– Pumice, Plantations and Power	32
	– Rotorua and Taupo	34
Tongariro National Park	– Gift to the Nation	36
Taranaki	– From the Mountain to the Sea	38
Whanganui and Manawatu	– From River to Plain	40
Wellington	– Capital City	42
	– Facing the Elements	44

Top of the South	– Sunny Marlborough and Nelson	**46**
West Coast	– Extraction v Conservation	**48**
	– Natural Forces at Work	**50**
Fiordland	– World Heritage Area	**52**
The Far South	– Oysters and Aluminium	**54**
Dunedin	– Edinburgh of the South	**56**
Central Otago	– Golden Heritage	**58**
Queenstown	– Adventure Capital	**60**
Mackenzie Country	– Tussock, Turbines and Tourists	**62**
Canterbury	– Patchwork Plains	**64**
Christchurch	– Mainland Capital	**66**
Southern Alps	– Crossing Over	**68**
	– High Country	**70**

61

52

31

Across the Water	– Island Lifestyles	**72**
	– Natural Sanctuaries	**74**
Quiz		**76**
Index		**78**
Sources & acknowledgements		**80**

63

New Zealand: An overview

A young country
New Zealand has come a long way in a short time. If the history of the world was a 400 m race, New Zealand would have joined in just before the finishing line.

On the move
Science and legend agree that New Zealand came up out of the sea. As it drifted away from the ancient super-continent of Gondwanaland it developed its own distinctive plants, animals and landscapes. As its young landforms are being built up by volcanic and tectonic forces they are being worn down by winds, waves, rivers and glaciers. New Zealand, trapped in an endless cycle of uplift and erosion, is a land on the move.

Human impact
Like any lively adolescent the people of New Zealand have taken risks, achieved some startling successes, and made many mistakes. The first New Zealanders arrived some 1000 years ago from Polynesia. Here they developed their unique Maori culture and left a lasting imprint on the land. A little over two hundred years ago Europeans came to New Zealand and the rate of change accelerated rapidly. Captain Cook would not recognise most of the country today, although so much of it is named by or after him.

Clean and green?
Much has been achieved in New Zealand but also much has been lost. At the end of the twentieth century, New Zealand was struggling to live up to its 'clean and green' image. Pollution, traffic jams, extinction, water shortages and soil erosion were all part of the New Zealand vocabulary. The kiwi, New Zealand's most popular icon, was down to only 5 per cent of its original numbers and its future threatened.

Signs of a greener future
At the dawn of the twenty-first century there are encouraging signs that New Zealanders are starting to take their environmental responsibilities more seriously. The first 'Green' politicians have been elected to Parliament and regional councils around the country are for the first time systematically measuring and reporting on the state of their environments. Like the emerging fight to save the kiwi, it is not a minute too soon.

New understandings
This book, like others to follow in the *Discovering New Zealand* series, is written for both New Zealanders and their many guests from around the world. Some of what they read will be familiar, some will be new; some things will surprise, others may amuse. Above all, it is hoped that readers will gain a desire to discover more about the people and places which make up New Zealand.

New Zealand: a brief chronology

c1300 Archaeological evidence suggests Polynesian settlement had begun by 1300.

1642 Dutch explorer Abel Tasman sights New Zealand but does not land. New Zealand's written history begins with conflict as Tasman's crew clash with Maori.

1769 British explorer Captain James Cook claims New Zealand for Britain. Total Maori population estimated to be between 100,000 and 200,000. Most live in warmer, coastal areas of North Island.

1790s European sealers and whalers arrive. Flax and timber trade begins and temporary settlements established around the coast. Maori suffer from first introduced disease epidemic.

1800s First European women arrive. Trade between European and Maori increases.

1810s Christian missionaries arrive. Sheep, cattle, horses and chickens introduced. First European child born.

1820s Hongi Hika, a Ngapuhi chief, visits England and returns via Sydney with muskets. Maori musket wars cause major upheaval in tribal relations. Many tribal areas temporarily abandoned.

1830s Whaling stations established and British Resident appointed to bring some law and order. Northern tribes sign Declaration of Independence. The New Zealand Company formed in London to organise British settlement in New Zealand.

1840s Treaty of Waitangi signed in Bay of Islands. Britain gains sovereignty, but Maori retain their land and other possessions. European settlements established at Wellington, New Plymouth, Wanganui, Nelson, Dunedin and Christchurch. War between British and Hone Heke and northern tribes. New settlements dependent on food and other resources supplied by local Maori.

1850s First national population census finds European population (about 60,000) has overtaken Maori population. Representative government (Europeans only) begins in the New Zealand colony. Maori resistance to land sales increases and first Maori king crowned. Sheep farming becomes established in South Island.

1860s Settler demands for land lead to war in the North Island. Large areas of Maori land are confiscated and Maori economic base destroyed. Gold rushes begin. First road taken across Southern Alps. Capital moves from Auckland to Wellington.

1870s Shipping, telegraph and railway developments as New Zealand's economy progresses. National system of primary education introduced. Armed conflict with Maori ends.

1880s Peaceful land protests by Maori, but Queen Victoria refuses to hear Maori king's concerns about land. First National Park is gifted to nation by Ngati Tuwharetoa.

1890s All men and women given the vote for the first time. (A world-first for women.) Maori establish an alternative parliament. North Island's population overtakes South Island's for first time. New Zealand troops fight for British in South Africa.

1900s Public Health Act is passed. First All Black rugby tour of Britain takes place. Main trunk railway line from Auckland to Wellington is completed. New Zealand becomes a Dominion. Ernest Rutherford wins Nobel Prize for Chemistry.

1910s Miners and waterfront workers strike. New Zealand joins Britain to fight in the First World War. ANZACs take part in Gallipoli campaign. Six o'clock closing of pubs only introduced.

1920s First flights across Cook Strait and Tasman Sea. The Depression begins.

1930s Hawke's Bay earthquake kills 256. Unemployment soars, relief work organised and large pine forests planted. First woman MP and then first Labour Government elected. Welfare State reforms provide state houses, national health service and 40-hour working week. New Zealand joins Britain to fight in the Second World War.

1940s Second World War continues until 1945. New Zealand signs United Nations charter and soon after becomes a fully independent nation. Protests against exclusion of Maori players from All Black rugby tour to apartheid South Africa.

1950s New Zealand signs defence agreements with allies (ANZUS, SEATO) and its troops fight in Korea and Malaya. Bitter Waterfront Strike. Major hydro-electric power schemes begin as population reaches two million. Hillary climbs Everest.

1960s Regular television and Cook Strait ferry services begin. New Zealand enters Vietnam conflict. Oil refinery and steel mill opened. The *Wahine* ferry sinks, killing 51. Pubs stay open until 10 p.m. and blood and breath testing introduced for drinking drivers.

1970s Britain's membership of EEC and first oil shock cause major economic problems. Protests over French nuclear testing in the Pacific, rugby with 'apartheid' South Africa and Maori land issues. Waitangi Tribunal established.

1980s Increasing protests over French nuclear testing, rugby with South Africa and Maori land issues. *Rainbow Warrior* sunk in Auckland harbour by French terrorists as New Zealand becomes nuclear-free. Waitangi Tribunal investigates Maori land claims back to 1840. Major social and economic reforms begin. Sunday shopping starts.

1990s Economic and social reforms continue and the Welfare State is dismantled. Maori land claims settled with Ngai Tahu and Tainui tribes. Auckland faces major problems with power, water supply, traffic and waste disposal. Electoral system reorganised and first Greens elected to Parliament.

2000s New Zealand leads the world into the 'new millennium'.

New Zealand: at a glance
Total Population: 3,681,546

EXPORT EARNINGS

- Services 25%
- Dairy Products 14%
- Crude Materials 14%
- Meat 10%
- Wood 9%
- Machinery/Transport 6%
- Seafood 4%
- Other food products 8%
- Other manufactured products 10%

ETHNIC GROUPS

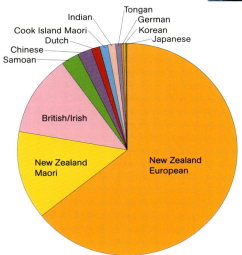

- New Zealand European
- New Zealand Maori
- British/Irish
- Samoan
- Chinese
- Cook Island Maori
- Dutch
- Indian
- Tongan
- German
- Korean
- Japanese

URBAN/RURAL SPLIT

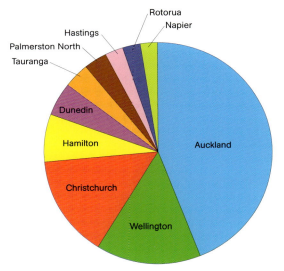

- Auckland
- Wellington
- Christchurch
- Hamilton
- Dunedin
- Tauranga
- Palmerston North
- Hastings
- Rotorua
- Napier

PASTORAL FARMING: LIVESTOCK NUMBERS

Sheep 47,394,000
Beef Cattle 4,852,000
Dairy Cattle 4,165,000
Deer 1,192,000
Pigs 424,000
Goats 228,000

ANNUAL TEMPERATURE

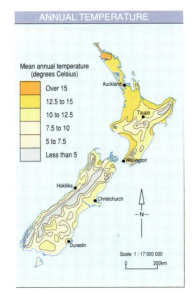

Mean annual temperature (degrees Celsius)
- Over 15
- 12.5 to 15
- 10 to 12.5
- 7.5 to 10
- 5 to 7.5
- Less than 5

ANNUAL SUNSHINE

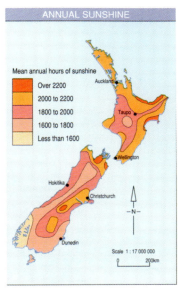

Mean annual hours of sunshine
- Over 2200
- 2000 to 2200
- 1800 to 2000
- 1600 to 1800
- Less than 1600

ANNUAL RAINFALL

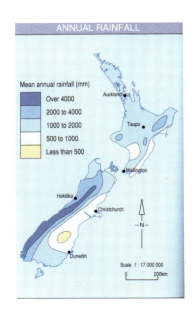

Mean annual rainfall (mm)
- Over 4000
- 2000 to 4000
- 1000 to 2000
- 500 to 1000
- Less than 500

NORTH ISLAND

Northland – Birthplace of a Nation

Spectacular sandhills guard the entrance to Hokianga Harbour, originally named Hokianga-nui-o-Kupe, the place of Kupe's great return. Today the harbour and sandhills attract tourists from all around the world.

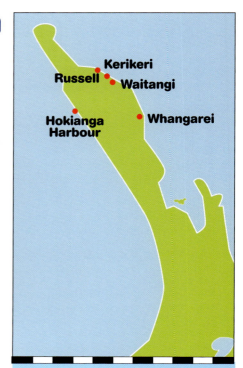

Northland, New Zealand's northern tip, is rich in history. As the cradle of both Maori and European settlement in New Zealand, it is considered by many to be the birthplace of the nation.

Tangata whenua

Maori legends tell the story of their ancestor Kupe, the Polynesian navigator. He discovered New Zealand over 1000 years ago when he sailed into Northland's Hokianga Harbour. After exploring the North Island he set sail from Hokianga to return to Hawaiki. He told his people about his discovery – Aotearoa, the land of the long white cloud.

It is said that many years later, Kupe's descendants left Hawaiki in ocean-going canoes in search of Aotearoa. Maori tribes (tangata whenua, the local people) trace their ancestry back to those canoes from Hawaiki, their ancestral home.

Pakeha

In 1769, James Cook, an English naval captain, became the first Pakeha (Maori term for European) to land on New Zealand's shores. His glowing descriptions of the country and its people soon attracted European sealers, whalers, traders, missionaries and settlers.

Like Kupe before him Captain Cook did not settle in New Zealand, but many of his people did soon after. By 1830 there were about 300 (mainly British) Pakeha living in New Zealand, many of them in the Bay of Islands. Here, many Maori profited from selling food, flax, timber and land to Pakeha. Payment was usually in the form of blankets, tobacco, nails and muskets.

New Zealand's oldest *stone* building, The Stone Store, built in 1835. Kemp House, built in 1822, is New Zealand's oldest building.

QUICK FACTS:
- Both Maori and Pakeha first settled in Northland on their arrival in New Zealand.
- British and Maori signed the Treaty of Waitangi in 1840.
- There were two different versions of 'the Treaty'.
- The Treaty is the cause of both celebration and protest.
- Today 32 per cent of Northlanders are Maori.

TIMELINE

AD 950 (approx.)
Kupe discovers Aotearoa

1300-1500
Main period of Polynesian settlement

1769
Captain Cook reaches New Zealand

1840
Treaty of Waitangi signed

1841
Capital moves from Russell to Auckland

1844-46
War between northern tribes and British

Conflict

By 1840 about 2000 Pakeha lived in New Zealand, but there was no official government or police force to keep the peace. Some unruly Pakeha had been causing trouble with Maori. Northern Maori tribes, armed with muskets traded from Pakeha, had been slaughtering enemy tribes to the south. New Zealand was becoming a dangerous place, and settlers and some Maori turned to the British Government for help.

With the Pakeha population severely outnumbered by about 100,000 Maori, the British Government was happy to seek a peaceful solution. After hurried negotiations between the British and Maori, a treaty was signed at Waitangi, in the Bay of Islands, in 1840. Some Maori leaders present argued against the Treaty, but most signed.

Waitangi

When the Treaty of Waitangi was signed both sides believed they had much to gain from sharing New Zealand. Maori ownership of the land was to be protected, the British could settle and the British Government would provide law and order for all.

There were, however, two versions of the Treaty of Waitangi. The English version was different from the Maori version. Most Maori signed the Maori version which promised them greater protection than the English version. Today, Maori own only a small fraction of their lands and the true meaning of the Treaty is still being argued.

Waitangi National Reserve preserves the history of the Treaty of Waitangi. In 1990, both celebration and protest marked the one hundred and fiftieth anniversary of the signing of what New Zealanders refer to as 'the Treaty'.

Russell

Russell became New Zealand's first capital in 1840, after the signing of the Treaty of Waitangi. Local Maori reacted angrily when, in 1841, the capital moved to Auckland. For them it meant a loss of trade and mana (prestige).

In 1844, Hone Heke, who had earlier signed the Treaty of Waitangi, cut down the British flagstaff above Russell. This act of protest was followed by an attack on the town and a two-year war with the British.

Russell.

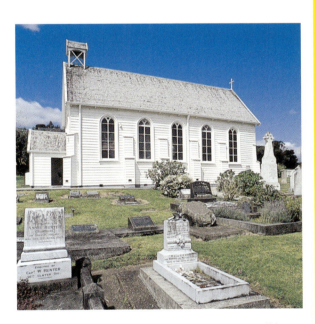
Bullet holes from Hone Heke's attack on Russell in 1844 can still be seen in the walls of Christ's Church. They are a reminder of the town's stormy past.

End of an era

The new nation of New Zealand had gotten off to a shaky start, but after 'Heke's War', Northland became a relatively quiet backwater. Auckland, the lower North Island and the South Island now attracted most of the new settlers.

NORTH ISLAND

DID YOU KNOW?

- **Russell**, scenic and respectable today, was reputed to be the 'hell-hole of the Pacific' in the 1830s. Then called Kororareka, it was notorious for drunkenness, violence and prostitution. In 1841, when Auckland became the new capital, Kororareka was given the name 'Russell' to try and improve its image. It seems to have worked!
- **Kerikeri**, in 1810, witnessed a plough being used for the first time in New Zealand. British missionary John Butler's historic ploughing is still commemorated in an annual ploughing competition. The award is a silver replica of Butler's plough.
- **Hongi Hika**, better known for his fighting qualities and brutal slaughter of rival tribes, helped missionaries set up mission stations on his land, visited Sydney and London, met King George IV, and even helped compile a Maori dictionary.
- **Hone Heke's** war with the British saw a rise in the Maori demand for Bibles. This pleased the missionaries until they found musket cartridges made out of their holy scriptures!
- **British soldiers** finally defeated Hone Heke and his ally, Kawiti, at Ruapekapeka pa on a Sunday. Believing their enemy to be Christian, the Maori defenders of the pa relaxed their guard. Caught out by the guns rather than the prayers of the British, they abandoned their pa and retreated into the forest.
- **New Zealand's** first road was built in Northland (between Kerikeri and Waimate North) in 1830, but Northland remained cut off by road from the rest of New Zealand until the 1930s – more than 100 years later!

NORTH ISLAND

Northland – The Winterless North

For many New Zealanders Cape Reinga is New Zealand's 'Land's End'. For Maori it is more significant at 'life's end'. The cape marks the point where the spirits of those who have died depart for their ancestral homeland, Hawaiki.

Northland's mild winters and hot summers attract visitors all year round and help grow a range of subtropical fruits. With no road link to the rest of New Zealand until the 1930s, Northland's development has for a long time been focused on the sea.

QUICK FACTS:
- Northland enjoys a subtropical climate.
- Cape Reinga is Northland's most famous landmark.
- Farming and tourism are the mainstays of the Northland economy.
- The Bay of Islands is the centre of Northland's many tourist attractions.
- Whangarei is Northland's main town.

Bay of Islands
Sparkling sea, 150 islands and a delightful climate make the Bay of Islands a marine paradise for thousands of New Zealanders and overseas visitors.

Majestic and ancient
Northland was once clothed in forests of kauri, a majestic conifer with an ancestry going back to the days of the dinosaur and Gondwanaland. During the nineteenth and early twentieth centuries nearly all

EVENTS CALENDAR:

January:
Bay of Islands Tall Ships Race
February:
6th, Waitangi Day celebrations at Waitangi National Reserve
March:
Northland Agricultural Field Days (New Zealand's second largest)
April:
Annual Kumara Festival, Dargaville
October:
Coastal Classic yacht race from Auckland to Russell

Whaling, which was important in the nineteenth century, has since been replaced by shipbuilding, commercial fishing, deep-sea game fishing, pleasure cruising and sailing, scuba diving and even swimming with dolphins!

Northland's kauri forests were converted into ships, homes and furniture. Fossilised gum from ancient kauri trees gave rise to a gum-digging industry that lasted for about one hundred years, peaking around 1900.

The Bay of Islands extends from Piercy Island at Cape Brett, with its famous 'hole in the rock', to historic Kerikeri Inlet.

Kerikeri's famous orange orchards are hidden from the view of the passing motorist by a maze of shelter-belt hedges.

The remarkable Kauri Museum at Matakohe records both the engineering feats and the environmental devastation of Northland's early kauri industry.

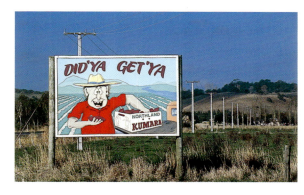

The kumara, a sweet potato, was introduced to New Zealand by its earliest Polynesian settlers. Dargaville, New Zealand's 'kumara capital', comes alive in April each year for its Kumara Festival.

Horticultural heaven

The far north's subtropical climate allows it to grow fruit and vegetables that do not grow well further south.

Postcard from Northland

Kia ora!

Northland is something else! Nearly slipped off NZ at Cape Reinga and surfed down the huge Hokianga sandhills — wow! They should have filmed Jurassic Park at Waipoua Kauri Forest. Those incredible trees would have made the dinosaurs look like toys.

There's so much history everywhere you go. The Waitangi war canoe was awesome, not to mention the paddlers!

Can't wait to come back — think I'll try swimming with the dolphins next time!

Love
Susie

Tane Mahuta (God of the Forest) is estimated to be 1200 years old. Over 50 m tall and 13 m around its trunk, it is one of the largest kauri in the Waipoua Forest.

NORTH ISLAND

DID YOU KNOW?

- **The Far North**, paradise to tourists, is also one of New Zealand's most disadvantaged areas with substandard housing and high unemployment.
- **Northland's** Kaipara Harbour is the largest harbour in New Zealand, stretching 70 km from Helensville in the south to Dargaville in the north.
- **A sunken** Spanish galleon, thought to lie hidden under the sands of Northland's Kauri Coast, has been linked to Maori legends about a fair-skinned race that arrived before Abel Tasman and Captain Cook.
- **Northland's** Ninety Mile Beach is only 64 miles (103 km) in length!
- **American author** Zane Grey made game fishing in the Bay of Islands world famous. He caught his first marlin here in 1926 and later bought an island in the Bay.
- **The *Rainbow Warrior*,** a Greenpeace ship sunk by French secret agents in Auckland in 1985, is now a sunken 'reef' for divers off Northland's Matauri Bay.
- **75 per cent** of New Zealand's remaining kauri trees are found in Waipoua Forest, some up to 2000 years old.
- **Despite** strong lobbying by conservationists since 1915, Northland's unique kauri forests still do not have National Park status.
- **Waipu**, settled by Scottish immigrants in the nineteenth century, has celebrated its heritage with annual 'Highland Games' since the 1870s.
- **Marsden Point**, New Zealand's only oil refinery, is situated on the west side of Whangarei Harbour. Each year it processes five million tonnes of crude oil.

NORTH ISLAND

Auckland – City of Sails

Westhaven Marina, Auckland.

QUICK FACTS:
- Auckland was established in 1840 and was the capital from 1841 until 1865.
- In 1996 greater Auckland had a population of 997,940.
- Auckland's Sky Tower is its most prominent building, but Rangitoto Island and One Tree Hill are its most famous landmarks.
- Auckland International Airport is New Zealand's main gateway.
- Auckland's economy is dominated by manufacturing, financial, tourist and social service industries.

EVENTS CALENDAR:

January:
Anniversary Day regatta on the Waitemata Harbour
March:
Annual 'Round the Bays' fun run
December:
Open-air 'Christmas in the Park' festival of music and entertainment

Auckland is New Zealand's largest city, home to nearly one third of the country's population. Hemmed in by sea, forest and 48 volcanoes, Auckland is now spilling over on to nearby islands and rich farming areas to the north and south. It has always been a desirable place to live.

Prime real estate

To pre-European Maori, Tamaki (as Auckland was then known) was a place 'desired by a hundred lovers' – Tamaki makau rau. Attracted by its gentle climate, rich volcanic soils, nearby forests and sheltered harbours, tribes constantly competed for this piece of 'prime real estate'.

In 1840, soon after the signing of the Treaty of Waitangi, local Maori persuaded the British to move their capital from Russell to Tamaki. In doing so they hoped to prevent further attacks by rival tribes. Governor Hobson named the new capital 'Auckland', after his friend Lord Auckland, then British Viceroy in India.

Governor Hobson purchased the original site of Auckland from local Maori in 1840. He paid £55 and an assortment of blankets, tobacco, clothing and food for a triangle of land stretching from the summit of Maungawhau (Mount Eden) to the Waitemata Harbour. Most of the rest of the Auckland isthmus was purchased for European settlement over the next 25 years.

Sailing is a popular pastime for many Aucklanders.

Auckland's business

Auckland lost its capital status to Wellington within 25 years, but it soon became New Zealand's leading commercial and industrial centre. Today, Auckland's economic dominance remains unchallenged.

Traditional heavy manufacturing industries are concentrated in the older suburbs of Onehunga, Penrose and Mount Wellington. More recently, estates of 'high-tech' light industry have displaced the orchards of Albany in the north and the dairy farms of East Tamaki in the south.

From sales to sails

Auckland's wealth and its spectacular Waitemata Harbour and Hauraki Gulf have combined to produce one of the highest rates of yacht ownership in the world. With an estimated rate of one boat for every four people it is no wonder that Auckland is known as the 'City of Sails'. A mild sunny climate, plenty of breeze, sheltered seas and a generous sprinkling of beautiful islands make Auckland a yachtie's haven.

People's parks

For those who can afford it, sailing is the perfect escape from Auckland's hustle and bustle and motorway madness. For others, Auckland offers a superb range of beaches and parks for its people to enjoy, free of charge.

From the lush bush of the Waitakere Ranges to the shining sands and shallow seas of Long Bay; from the wild west's cliff-top colony of gannets to the silent grandeur of Rangitoto Island, Auckland's local, maritime and regional parks provide something for everyone.

Changing places

For many Aucklanders the dream of a spacious suburban home appears to be fading. Motorway traffic jams and a new café culture are making inner-city apartment living more attractive for some young urban professionals.

NORTH ISLAND

DID YOU KNOW?

- **When** the Auckland Harbour Bridge (which opened in 1959) became too small for the number of vehicles using it, the extra lanes fitted by a Japanese construction company in 1969 became known as the 'Nippon clip-ons'.
- **Auckland** region is made up of four cities and two districts: Auckland City, Manukau City, Waitakere City, North Shore City, Franklin District and Rodney District.
- **The built-up** area of Auckland stretches 50 km from Long Bay in the north to Drury in the south.
- **Auckland** is built on and around 48 different volcanoes. Although no individual volcano is currently active, vulcanologists confidently expect further eruptions to occur in the Auckland volcanic field. (See City of Volcanoes, pages 16-17.)
- **Auckland** has a multicultural population. According to the 1996 census about one quarter of the population was either Maori or of Pacific Island descent, making Auckland the largest Polynesian city in the world. (See Pacific City, pages 18-19.)

NORTH ISLAND

Auckland – City of Volcanoes

Sleek and symmetrical, Rangitoto is Auckland's youngest and largest volcano. It is thought to have erupted about 600 years ago. Now protected by the Department of Conservation, Rangitoto was once the site of a prison quarry and an American naval base.

QUICK FACTS:

- Oldest volcano – Auckland Domain, erupted about 100,000 years ago.
- Youngest volcano – Rangitoto, erupted about 600 years ago.
- Largest volcano – Rangitoto, contains a third of all lava in Auckland.
- Highest volcano – Mount Eden, 196 m.

New Zealand, the home of bungy jumping and adventure tourism, also has a reputation for risky living. Its capital city is built on an active fault line and Auckland, its largest city, sprawls over and around 48 volcanoes! The Auckland volcanic field started erupting between 60,000 and 140,000 years ago and it shows no sign of losing its fiery habit. Vulcanologists cannot predict with any certainty where the next eruption will be, but they are certain of one thing – there will be another eruption!

Cones, craters, flows and tunnels

Auckland's volcanoes have created a varied and unique landscape. The better known of its volcanoes such as Maungakiekie (One Tree Hill), Maungawhau (Mount Eden) and Maungarei (Mount Wellington) rise proudly above the Auckland landscape.

Mount Hobson: This volcanic cone was formed when a 'fire fountain' of gassy lava piled up deposits of scoria around its vent. Only when all the gas had been released did lava flow freely and make its way down existing valleys towards the sea.

Lake Pupuke: Volcanic eruptions by the sea tended to explode violently as rising magma came into contact with water. Large explosion craters were formed, many filling later with water. Lake Pupuke is a fine example.

Meola Reef: Auckland's longest lava flow extends from Mount Roskill to the sea at Point Chevalier. Here it continues as Meola Reef, reaching almost to the far side of the Waitemata Harbour at Birkenhead, a distance of over 10 km.

One Tree Hill.

16

NORTH ISLAND

DID YOU KNOW?

- **Auckland's** volcanoes are thought to be caused by a hot spot – a large mass of red-hot magma held in the earth's crust. Every so often a 'bubble' of magma breaks free and erupts lava onto the Auckland landscape.
- **All Aucklanders** should know what to do in the event of a volcanic eruption. Every home should have a disaster survival kit.
- **Terraces** cut by Maori into the steep slopes of Auckland's volcanic cones were once known as Nga Wakairo a Titahi, the carvings of the warrior chief Titahi. The terraces provided narrow strips of flat land for houses and food stores.
- **Meola Reef** has several times been considered as a natural place to bridge the Waitemata Harbour. Maori legends tell of a fairy people who tried to do just that. Afraid of the light, they built the reef by night. In their excitement, as they neared the far shore they failed to notice the approaching dawn. Trapped on the reef by the sun's first rays they perished and the bridge was never finished.
- **Rangitoto** is not only Auckland's youngest volcano but also its largest. It contains one third of all Auckland's lava. How big will the next eruption be?
- **The original** 'tree' of One Tree Hill was a native totara, and sacred to Maori. It was cut down for firewood by a Pakeha settler last century, and replaced by a pine tree. Chainsaw attacks on the pine tree by Maori protesters in the 1990s may hasten the return of a totara tree to the summit.

Using Auckland's volcanoes

Auckland's volcanoes have been valued by people ever since human occupation began there. Maori used them as defensive sites and their soils for horticulture. Europeans have used them as quarries, parks, tourist attractions, rock climbing venues, exclusive building sites, reservoirs and even sewage works!

Mount Eden: For pre-European Maori the cones provided excellent defensive sites for their fortified pa. Maungawhau's defences were breached on one occasion only after a lengthy siege – it had no permanent water supply. Ironically, Maungawhau now has a large reservoir built into its flanks and supplies high-pressure water to the surrounding suburbs.

Mount Wellington: Lava flows from Maungarei were blocked by earlier flows and a deep 'lake' of lava formed. In the 1930s this solidified mass of lava, 30 m deep, became the site of a quarry. Supplying much of the rock needed for Auckland's motorways and international airport, the Mount Wellington quarry was for a time the largest quarry in the southern hemisphere.

North Head: Standing on guard at the entrance to the Waitemata Harbour, North Head has been a military base for over 100 years. The volcanic cone is riddled with secret tunnels, bunkers and gun emplacements.

One Tree Hill: Maungakiekie and its surrounding slopes are now preserved as One Tree Hill Domain and Cornwall Park. This famous Auckland landmark, little damaged by quarrying, is an inner-city haven of beauty and serenity – the domain of picnickers, joggers and grazing sheep.

NORTH ISLAND

Auckland – Pacific City

Hundreds of young Aucklanders gather at the annual Secondary Schools Cultural Festival to celebrate the city's colourful and vibrant Pacific cultures.

QUICK FACTS:
- Maori make up 10 per cent of Auckland's population.
- Pacific Islanders make up 13 per cent of Auckland's population.
- Auckland is the largest Polynesian city in the world.

EVENTS CALENDAR:
March:
Pasifika Festival, Secondary Schools Cultural Festival
November:
Eden-Albert Primary Schools Cultural Festival

Auckland is often referred to as the Polynesian capital of the world. Maori trace their ancestry back to Hawaiki in ancient Polynesia. A modern wave of migration from Polynesia began in the 1950s. Today Auckland is home to more Niueans than live in Niue, and also has thriving communities of Samoans, Cook Islanders and Tongans.

Education

Auckland's schools take pride in their students' Polynesian heritage. Maori language and culture is taught in most schools and many have their own marae and meeting house. Children can be educated in the Maori language from preschool classes through to a secondary school. Kohanga reo, Maori language nests, foster Maori language and culture for preschool children. Their success has encouraged Pacific Island communities to set up their own 'language nests' and help keep their cultures alive for New Zealand-born generations.

From an early age children of all cultures have opportunities to share in Auckland's rich cultural heritage. The annual Eden-Albert Cultural Festival attracts hundreds of enthusiastic and talented dancers from local primary and intermediate schools.

Arts

Maori and Pacific artists are helping to change the face of Auckland. Their art is prominently displayed at popular venues and is appreciated by visitors to New Zealand. Maori artist Ralph Hotere's spectacular work welcomes visitors to Auckland's Sky Tower.

Each year Auckland's Pacific communities gather at the Pasifika Festival held by the lake at Western Springs to celebrate their distinctive art, music and food — their Pacific way of life.

Pacific designs and designers are making an impact on the way Aucklanders dress and furnish their homes.

Out and about

A summer weekend at Auckland's Long Bay Regional Park, or the Otara flea market in South Auckland, are the closest you can get to Apia, Avarua or Nuku'alofa without leaving Auckland. The energy, creativity and community spirit of Auckland's Polynesian community is there for all to experience.

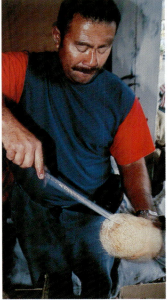

This scene at the Otara flea market could just as easily be taking place somewhere in the Pacific Islands. Pacific cultures are strongly Christian and much of their community life in New Zealand revolves around church activities. Traditional white clothing and inspirational singing are very much a part of Pacific Island church life in New Zealand.

Sport

Sport is probably the area in which Auckland's Pacific character is most strongly represented, from traditional rugby to new arrivals like kilikiti and outrigger canoe racing. Increasingly our netball, rugby and rugby league heroes are Maori and Polynesian.

No All Black rugby test at Eden Park would be complete without the traditional pre-match Maori haka, a vigorous challenge to the opposing team. Tongan-born Aucklander Jonah Lomu is one of several Polynesians to star in recent All Black teams.

Enthusiasts of all cultures compete in Polynesian-inspired outrigger canoes on Auckland's Waitemata Harbour.

European missionaries took cricket to the Pacific and it has come back Pacific-style. What Pacific Islanders did to cricket was mirrored many years later in the one-day cricket revolution — it became faster, noisier and much more colourful!

NORTH ISLAND

DID YOU KNOW?

- **The Polynesian** triangle stretches from New Zealand in the south to Tahiti in the northeast and Hawaii in the north. Polynesian cultures and languages can be traced back to common origins. New Zealand Maori can usually be understood by Cook Islanders. 'Haere ra' (goodbye) in New Zealand Maori is 'Aere ra' in Cook Island Maori.
- **Polynesian** ancestors are thought to have migrated eastwards from Malaysia and Indonesia and island-hopped through to modern Polynesia. New Zealand was the last and the largest of the Polynesian islands to be settled.
- **New Zealand** annexed the Cook Islands and Niue in 1901, and took over from German rule in Western Samoa when the First World War broke out in 1914.
- **Cook Islanders,** Niueans and Tokelauans are New Zealand citizens.
- **The Cook Island** parliament has a member (MP) to represent Cook Islanders living in the electorate of New Zealand.

New Zealand – a Pacific nation

The national identity of New Zealanders is no longer dominated by British culture. They see their country as a distinctively Pacific nation, and Auckland as a Pacific city. Wellington may be the capital of New Zealand, but for many, Auckland is the capital of Polynesia.

NORTH ISLAND

Coromandel – Heart of Gold

Coastline near Port Jackson, Coromandel Peninsula.

Coromandel's past has caught up with it again. Gold, first discovered there in 1850, is back and Coromandel is at a crossroads. Does its future lie in tourism and its natural beauty, or does it bring in the excavators and mine the gold? Conservation or exploitation? Coromandel has tried both over the past 100 years.

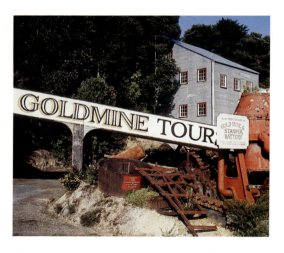

Coromandel is rich in minerals. The discovery of gold at Thames in 1850 eventually led to a gold rush in the 1860s, attracting fortune-seekers from around the world. Within ten years the easily accessible gold in the Thames goldfields had been extracted and the miners left as quickly as they had come. Only at Waihi's Martha Hill mine did significant gold mining continue. Closed in 1952, the mine reopened on a much larger open-cast scale in 1988.

The narrow and rugged peninsula was stripped of its majestic kauri trees and plundered for gold in an uncontrolled frenzy of nineteenth century exploitation. People and towns came and went as fortunes were made and lost.

A century later the scars had healed and Coromandel was rediscovering its spectacular natural attractions. It was a haven for alternative lifestylers and bach-owners. A tourist industry was emerging, offering the twin attractions of outstanding natural beauty and the peninsula's mining and logging heritage. Coromandel's conservation seemed assured. Now the gold miners are back, encouraged by the high price of gold and armed with technology that allows them to literally move mountains. Which way will Coromandel go?

Forestry

From the 1870s for a period of 40 years, the once majestic kauri forests of the Coromandel were felled to build the Victorian villa suburbs of cities in New Zealand and Australia.

QUICK FACTS:
- Moehau at 892 m is the peninsula's highest point.
- The climate varies greatly from the wet west to the sunnier east.
- Tourism, forestry, farming, fishing and gold mining are the mainstays of Coromandel's economy.
- The main towns are Thames, Coromandel, Waihi and Whangamata.

EVENTS CALENDAR:

July (varies each year):
Annual Waihi Miners' Stampede – wheelbarrow race
November:
Festival of the Environment – 'green' activities

The energy, endurance and ingenuity of Coromandel's kauri loggers was as remarkable as it was devastating to the Coromandel environment.

Natural delights

Coromandel's rugged mountain backbone attracts trampers and campers from around the world, while its golden east coast beaches and offshore islands provide for more leisurely pursuits. The northern peninsula is a haven for the independent traveller looking to get off the beaten track. Further south the irresistible attractions of sun, sand and surf swell the summer populations of resort towns Whangamata and Waihi Beach.

Thousands of summer swimmers and surfers are attracted to the Coromandel's best surf beaches. Local surf lifesaving clubs provide a 'vital' service keeping people safe in the water.

Historic towns

Coromandel's nineteenth century gold mining heritage is well preserved in the townships of Thames and Coromandel. Victorian architecture (no doubt built from local kauri timber) provides the charm, and small museums and working exhibits recall the exploits of the gold-rush days.

Remote huts and riverside campsites around the popular Kauaeranga Valley attract the more adventurous holidaymaker.

Hot Water Beach, Coromandel: free hot spas are available at low tide – just bring a shovel!

Postcard from Coromandel

Hi there!

Was taken round an old gold mine at Thames — you should have seen those huge weta insects! Freaky!! Proud to say I got to the top of the Pinnacles this afternoon — what a view from the top, but I had to hang on tight as there wasn't much room up there. This place must have been incredible before the kauri trees were cut down. Still, there are some big ones left — we saw the 'square kauri'. Its trunk really is square!
Heading for Hot Water Beach tomorrow to soak my weary legs!

Bye for now
Jim

NORTH ISLAND

DID YOU KNOW?

- **According** to Maori legend, Tama-te-kapua, chief of the Arawa canoe, is buried on top of Moehau, the Coromandel's highest point. Today it is a sacred reserve.
- **The remarkable** Archey's frog lives high on the Coromandel Peninsula, away from open water. It does not have webbed feet and its young do not become tadpoles – they grow from eggs to adults!
- **Captain Cook** named Mercury Bay and the offshore Mercury Islands after witnessing the Transit of Mercury in the night sky there on 4 November 1769.
- **Coromandel** was probably named after HMS *Coromandel*, which shipped kauri spars from the peninsula in 1820. The original Coromandel coast is in south-east India.
- **Silence** is golden? In 1871 more than 70 gold mines were operating around Thames. At night the town reverberated to the sound of 40 stamper batteries crushing the quartz rock to release its gold.
- **The Coromandel Peninsula** contains many other minerals, apart from gold. It is a haven for gemstone collectors. Jasper, agate, onyx and even opals have been found there.
- **Dams** (to flush out felled logs) and booms (to stop them washing out to sea) were examples of remarkable bush engineering which allowed nineteenth century loggers to extract kauri from the remote and rugged mountains of the Coromandel. The famous 'Billy Goat' tramline, which by-passed the towering and log-smashing Billy Goat waterfalls, was another.

NORTH ISLAND

Waikato – From Cowbells to Caverns

The Waikato region, named after the mighty river of the same name (see pages 24-25), has been at the heart of New Zealand's social and economic development.

QUICK FACTS:
- The Waikato administrative region is the fourth largest in the country, extending from Tongariro National Park in the south to the outer suburbs of Auckland in the north.
- Main towns and cities are Hamilton, Cambridge, Tokoroa and Taupo.
- Its economy is dominated by dairying, mining, forestry and tourism.
- There are over one million cows in about 5000 dairy herds in the Waikato.

EVENTS CALENDAR:
April:
Balloons Over Waikato, hot air ballooning event, Hamilton
June:
NZ Agricultural Fieldays, Mystery Creek

In the 1840s and 1850s Waikato Maori provided most of the timber and food needs of a growing Auckland. They milled timber, raised pigs, grew vegetables and wheat, owned flour mills and ships, and carried on a valuable trade with Pakeha settlers.

By 1860 a flood of new settlers was demanding land and a 'slice of the business action'. Waikato tribes would not sell their land so the settler government decided to take it. Governor Grey provoked a war in which overwhelming British military power eventually brought them victory. In 1863 Waikato tribes were 'punished' for their resistance by the confiscation of their land. Many Waikato Maori retreated south to the hilly 'King Country' when their confiscated land was shared out amongst Pakeha soldiers and settlers.

On 20-21 November 1863, Rangiriri pa was the site of a decisive battle in the Waikato Land Wars. Outnumbered, and severely bombarded by British cannons, 400 Maori could not sustain their brave resistance. Abandoning their pa overnight, about half escaped by canoe across the neighbouring Waikare wetland, and the rest were taken prisoner.

Dairy farming
By 1900 Pakeha development had cleared much of the Waikato's lowland forests and drained its swamps to make way for dairy farming. By the 1930s it had become New Zealand's leading dairying region, a rolling landscape of green paddocks and neat hedgerows. Small rural communities serviced local farmers and their families. It was claimed to be the richest dairying land in the world.

By the end of the twentieth century there were indications that dairying in the Waikato had been over-developed. Farms and dairy factories had become so large, mechanised and efficient that small rural communities were disappearing off the map. Concerns were also being raised about the environmental damage caused by too many cows and the excessive use of chemical fertilisers.

Hamilton

When Hamilton was established in 1864 soldiers in the Waikato Militia were each given 1.5 ha in the town and 20 ha in the country. Well-situated by the Waikato River, on State Highway 1 and the main trunk railway line, Hamilton has become New Zealand's fourth largest city. As well as servicing its farming hinterland, Hamilton has its own industries, excellent schools, university and research establishments.

Minerals

Massive dunes of black ironsand at the mouth of the Waikato River, and also further south at Taharoa, provide the raw material for iron and steel making at nearby Glenbrook Steel Mill and in Japan. Over 1.5 million tonnes of coal are produced each year by Waikato's coal mines.

The largest mines are at Huntly (underground) and Rotowaro (open cast). Worldwide concerns about the environmental effects of burning coal and other fossil fuels have cast some doubt over the long-term future of Waikato's coal mines.

Natural attractions

Waitomo Caves, 77 km south of Hamilton, penetrate deep into limestone hills. Most famous for the glittering wonders of its glow-worm cave, the caves offer opportunities for adventure – black-water rafting, abseiling into seemingly bottomless caverns and pot-holing.

Raglan is New Zealand's surfing mecca, and reputed to have the best left-handed break in the world. The surf is so good that the local college now offers youngsters from around the world a chance to surf-as-they-learn in its Surfing Academy.

NORTH ISLAND

DID YOU KNOW?

- **Hamilton**, 40 km from the sea and with a population of about 160,000, is New Zealand's largest inland city.
- **Hamilton** was named after a British naval commander killed in 1864 during the Waikato Land Wars. The original Maori village there was called Kirikiriroa.
- **Hamilton's** Candyland factory has featured in the *Guinness Book of Records* as the maker of the world's largest lollipop!
- **Coal** was first mined in the Waikato during the 1840s by a European missionary. During the Land Wars twenty years later, British gunboats on the Waikato River were fuelled by local coal.
- **The southern hemisphere's** largest agricultural field days are held at Mystery Creek near Hamilton each June. Attracting over 100,000 visitors, it is the premier showcase for New Zealand farming.

NORTH ISLAND

Waikato – A Powerful River

Waikato, known to Maori as the river of a hundred taniwha, today flows through eight hydroelectric power stations on its way from Lake Taupo to the Tasman Sea. It is indeed a powerful river.

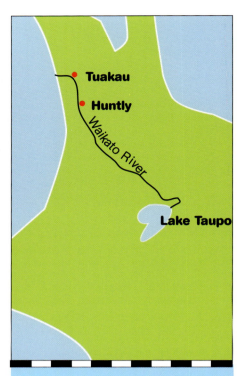

QUICK FACTS:
- New Zealand's longest river, 425 km.
- Headwaters on the slopes of Mount Ruapehu.
- Flows into the Tasman Sea at Port Waikato.
- Has eight hydroelectric power stations.

EVENTS CALENDAR:
February:
New Zealand Rowing Championships, Lake Karapiro (continues into March)
March:
Regatta Day at Ngaruawahia. Spectacular cultural performances on and off the river

The Waikato is New Zealand's longest river. Its waters reflect both the landscape and the history of New Zealand more than any other river.
- For centuries it gave Maori canoes access to the North Island's interior.
- During the Waikato Land Wars (see pages 22-23) it allowed British gunboats to bombard Maori pa from close range.
- Its hydroelectric power stations have powered the homes and industries of the upper North Island for over 70 years.
- Its present polluted state records not only the river's use, but also its abuse. Receiving regular doses of sewage, sediment and chemicals from farms, forestry and industry, the river's pollution presents a major challenge to the people of the Waikato.

History

Waikato tribes are united by their affiliation to the river. In 1858, at Ngaruawahia on the banks of the Waikato, Te Wherowhero became the first Maori king. Waikato tribes had united around their king to resist the loss of their land to Pakeha settlers. In 1863, after military defeat in the Waikato Land Wars, the King and his followers were forced to abandon their pa and retreat south to what is still known as the King Country. It wasn't until 1881, after the second Maori king, Tawhiao, made peace with the colonial government that his followers began to return to Ngaruawahia.

Taupiri is the sacred ancestral mountain of Waikato tribes. It has been used as an urupa (burial ground) for over a century, with those of highest status being buried nearest the summit.

Turangawaewae marae is the official residence of the present Maori queen. Built on the banks of the Waikato, it overlooks the site of the first king's pa. Every year on Regatta Day the marae is opened to the public and majestic waka take to the river in celebration.

Huka Falls.

Waikato's hydro schemes

Headwaters: Two power stations have been built on the headwaters of the Waikato which flow out of Tongariro National Park and into Lake Taupo.

Huka Falls: Tourists flock here to watch the Waikato thunder through a narrow chasm.

Atiamuri: This power station is one of eight built along the fast-flowing upper Waikato River between the 1920s and 1960s. Together they produce about 20 per cent of New Zealand's electricity.

Karapiro: The dam at Karapiro raised the river 30 m and created a lake 24 km in length. Lake Karapiro is a popular rowing venue, hosting the world championships in 1978.

Hamilton: A city both united and divided by the Waikato River and its five road bridges. A leisurely old-time paddle steamer which cruises the river is popular with tourists.

River mouth: 425 km from its farthest source, the Waikato drops its heavy load of sediment as it spills out into the Tasman Sea.

Huntly: The mainly coal-fired thermal power station at Huntly draws the water for its steam turbines from the Waikato. Commissioned in 1981, it can generate more electricity than the eight Waikato hydro stations combined!

Huntly Power Station.

Hamilton.

NORTH ISLAND

DID YOU KNOW?

• **Over 50 streams** and rivers flow into Lake Taupo but only one flows out of it – the Waikato.

• **The Tongariro River**, one of the headwaters of the Waikato River which flow into Lake Taupo, was called Waikato until it was officially renamed in 1945.

• **Until a major** Taupo eruption nearly 2000 years ago, the Waikato used to flow out to sea near Thames. Volcanic material from the eruption blocked its original course and diverted the river towards the Tasman Sea.

• **The Waikato Land Wars** could just have easily been known as the Waikato River Wars. The ability of British gunships (armoured paddle steamers) to attack Maori positions from the river, and their ability to deliver supplies to British troops, gave the British a decisive advantage in the war.

• **After Auckland's 1995** drought, water and water crisis plans were drawn up to pipe water from the Waikato River. This raised immediate concerns about the polluted state of the river.

• **Near Tuakau**, pumice sands are 'vacuumed' up from the Waikato River's bed by a suction dredge. The pumice is used for concrete products and for improving soil drainage.

• **Rowing** is a sport at which people from the Waikato excel. Helped by the superb facilities at Lake Karapiro, they consistently win national rowing championships.

• **Orakei Korako**, a spectacular geothermal wonderland on the shores of Lake Ohakuri/Waikato River, is accessible only by boat.

NORTH ISLAND

Bay Of Plenty – Kiwifruit Country

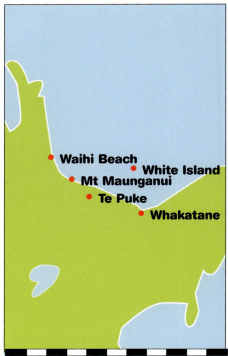

'We saw a great deal of cultivated land laid out in regular inclosures, a sure sign that the country is both fertile and well inhabited.' So said Captain Cook on 1 November 1769 when he first saw the Bay of Plenty. He could just as easily have been describing this modern day view of the 'the Bay' and its kiwifruit orchards. New Zealand produces 25 pert cent of the world's kiwifruit and 80 per cent of that is grown in the Bay of Plenty where the soils, climate and gentle slopes provide ideal growing conditions.

Te Puke, nestled towards the western end of the sunny Bay of Plenty, is the kiwifruit capital of the world. The kiwifruit was first cultivated in New Zealand in the 1920s but it wasn't until 1952 that a trial shipment was sent overseas. By the 1960s a kiwifruit 'boom' was under way and everyone seemed to be growing it. After a 'crash' at the end of the 1980s the kiwifruit industry is booming once again. It has returned with fewer growers, higher standards and a cleaner, greener, healthier reputation.

A single kiwifruit contains enough vitamin C to meet the daily needs of an adult. Some claim it reduces cholesterol, too. No wonder it is a popular health food overseas.

Kiwifruit originated in China, where they are known as monkey food, or mihoutao: they grow so high in the canopies of forest trees that only monkeys can reach them. Cultivated kiwifruit in New Zealand are trained over pergola structures and regularly pruned to keep the fruit at an easy picking height.

QUICK FACTS:

- The Bay of Plenty stretches over 150 km from Waihi Beach to beyond Opotiki.
- Main towns and cities are Tauranga, Mount Maunganui, Whakatane, Te Puke and Opotiki.
- The Bay enjoys a sunny, mild, though sometimes windy climate.
- A popular retirement place, the Bay has a higher average age than most other regions.
- Its population swells seasonally with summer holidaymakers and autumn kiwifruit pickers.

EVENTS CALENDAR:

April:
Kiwifruit-picking season begins
July:
Te Puke Kiwifruit Festival
September:
Woodskills Festival, Kawerau
October:
'King of the Mountain' race up and down Mount Edgecumbe

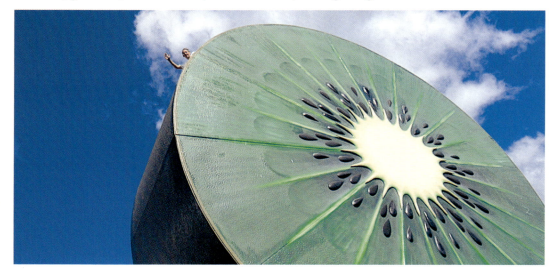

The 'Big Kiwifruit' at Te Puke leaves visitors in no doubt about which fruit is king of the Bay. The wild 'Chinese gooseberry' vine has been tamed and renamed in New Zealand to become a kiwi icon with a worldwide reputation.

A place for young and old

The gentle, sunny climate and the relative peace and quiet of the western Bay of Plenty attracts many of New Zealand's older citizens. Retirement homes and villages cluster around Tauranga and Mount Maunganui. It is also a mecca for young holidaymakers, drawn by the Bay's sun, surf and social activities. New Year celebrations can sometimes get out of hand and extra police from outside the region further boost the Bay's summer population.

With a rapidly ageing population, the growth of retirement homes outside Tauranga seems set to continue.

Earthquake!

At 1.42 p.m. on 2 March 1987 central Bay of Plenty rocked and rolled to the tune of a violent earthquake. Seven minutes before, a smaller shock had convinced teachers at Edgecumbe College to evacuate their classrooms. It's just as well they did as students were lined up on the school's playing fields when the big one struck. No one was seriously injured.

The 1987 Bay of Plenty earthquake measured only 6.3 on the Richter scale, but its focus was near enough to the surface to lift and shake a wide area. A seven kilometre fissure sliced across the Rangitaiki Plain, and stumps of an ancient forest were raised up out of the Rangitaiki River.

Volcano!

The Bay of Plenty is where the North Island's active volcanic zone slips into the sea. It is volcano country. Inland stands the extinct Mount Edgecumbe, and 51 km offshore lies smoking White Island. Geologists have recently discovered more erupting volcanoes on the sea floor much further out to sea. The threat of a tsunami from a major offshore eruption hangs over the entire bay.

White Island, now almost continuously active, was mined for sulphur until 1914 when an eruption and landslide destroyed the mine and killed all twelve miners.

'The Mount', as it is known to its summer visitors, provides just about everything a young holidaymaker could wish for. Lifeguards, wary of treacherous rip currents, keep a watchful eye on swimmers in the surf.

NORTH ISLAND

DID YOU KNOW?

- **The ancestral canoes** of two Maori tribes, Te Arawa and Mataatua, made final landfall along the Bay of Plenty's shores. The Arawa waka landed at Maketu and the Mataatua at Whakatane further to the east.
- **Whakatane** got its name when a woman saved the Mataatua canoe from drifting out to sea while the male paddlers were exploring ashore. Taking the initiative she cried out, 'Kia whakatane au I ahau'– 'I will act like a man.'
- **The Bay of Plenty** was named by Captain Cook in 1769. After the dry barrenness of Gisborne's Poverty Bay he was suitably impressed by the green fertility of this 'bay of plenty'.
- **Tauranga** and the western Bay of Plenty is the fastest-growing region in New Zealand, attracting in particular people aged 25 and over. Its economy is boosted by tourism, forestry, local agriculture and the country's second largest port at nearby Mount Maunganui.
- **Katikati**, one of the first Bay towns if you approach from the west, is known as New Zealand's 'mural town'. Professional artists have painted the history of Katikati in lifelike detail on the walls of the town's buildings. No stuffy art gallery or museum here!
- **Zespri Gold** is a new variety of kiwifruit developed by New Zealand scientists. It has a sweeter taste and yellow flesh.
- **Tasman Pulp and Paper Mill** at Kawerau earns millions of dollars for the Bay, and the name 'The Black Drain' for the Kawerau River. Chemical pollutants from the mill kill nearly all life in the river and stain it dark black.

NORTH ISLAND

East Cape – First to See the Sun

The East Cape received mainland New Zealand's first light of the new millennium on 1 January 2000.

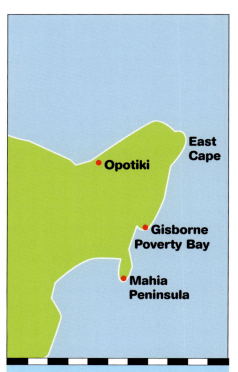

QUICK FACTS:
- The East Cape region extends from Opotiki to Gisborne.
- East Cape is the most easterly point of mainland New Zealand.
- Gisborne (population 33,000) is the only city in the region.
- The other main towns are Ruatoria and Wairoa.
- The economy is based on farming, forestry and tourism.

EVENTS CALENDAR:
January:
Gisborne – first city to see the sun each year
Tolaga Bay Beach Races
February:
Long Board Surf Classic, Makaorori Beach, Gisborne
October:
Wine and Food Festival, Gisborne

Mount Hikurangi is the highest point of the rugged Raukumara Range. It overlooks New Zealand's East Cape region. This remote shoulder of land, stretching from Opotiki to Gisborne, has its own distinctive character.

The first Europeans to set foot on New Zealand soil landed close to present day Gisborne. It was a bad start to Maori-Pakeha relations. After a brief encounter, Captain Cook and his *Endeavour* sailed away, leaving four Maori dead and calling the place Poverty Bay. Cook had misjudged the area's potential – it is in fact blessed with a beautiful climate and fertile plains.

Captain Cook must have been guessing when he named East Cape in 1769 as he hadn't been there before. He was drawing the first map of New Zealand as he went, but it did indeed prove to be the most easterly part of New Zealand.

Industrial ruins and a rotting wharf are evidence of better times at Tokomaru Bay. Cut off from the rest of New Zealand except by sea, Tokomaru Bay was one of several thriving settlements around East Cape until its freezing works closed in 1956 and people moved away.

Distinctively Maori

Apart from a period in the early 1900s when coastal shipping supported a thriving trade in meat and wool, the East Cape has attracted relatively little Pakeha interest or investment. It remains a distinctively Maori part of New Zealand today. Ngati Porou, the local iwi around the coast, are renowned for their carving skills and fine meeting houses. Inland, the forests of the Urewera have long protected the more isolated Tuhoe people. Both iwi have provided some of New Zealand's more remarkable spiritual, political and military leaders.

Te Kooti (c. 1830-1893) is remembered for both his spiritual and military achievements. He founded the Ringatu religious faith (which still has followers today) while imprisoned on the Chatham Islands in 1866. Escaping from the Chathams he led a guerrilla warfare campaign against the Government until 1872. He was eventually pardoned by the Government in 1883.

Rua Kenana (1869-1937) responded to the threatened loss of Tuhoe land by establishing an independent community deep in the Urewera forests at Maungapohatu in 1905. It had its own bank, parliament and religious beliefs. As a charismatic spiritual leader, Kenana helped his Tuhoe people resist the intrusion of Pakeha ways and the loss of their tribal land.

Sir Apirana Ngata

Sir Apirana Ngata (1874-1950) came from Ruatoria and became the first Maori to graduate from a New Zealand university. He went on to become a member of Parliament for 38 years. He is remembered for his lifelong commitment to improving the social and economic well-being of Maori.

Te Moananuiakiwa Ngarimu, VC (1913-1943) came from near Waipiro Bay and is proudly remembered as the first Maori to be awarded the Victoria Cross. During the Second World War he was decorated for his great skill and bravery while leading an attack on enemy machine-gun posts at Tebaga Gap, North Africa. He died from the wounds he received.

Soil slips away

Early European settlers in the East Cape cleared hills of their protective forests and sowed grass seed. For a while hill country sheep and beef farming was successful, but the thin covering of grass was unable to hold the soil when storms blew in from the sea. Rain rushed down the bare hillsides taking the soil with it. Farmers abandoned the land in the worst-affected areas. To stop the erosion plantations of fast-growing pine forests were established during the 1970s and 1980s. The East Cape now has a growing timber industry, but its fragile hills still need careful management.

By the time Cyclone Bola smashed into the East Cape in 1988 less than one third of its fragile hills had been reforested. Devastating erosion in the hills and flooding in the valleys caused $112 million worth of damage. It was a shocking reminder that East Cape's steep hills need their forests.

Gisborne

Gisborne grabbed the attention of the world when it became the first city in the world to see the sun on New Year's Day, 2000. Despite its name, Poverty Bay is rich in natural resources. Its warm, sunny climate and fertile plains produce a wide range of horticultural produce, including some of New Zealand's finest wines. The relatively few tourists who reach Gisborne discover what surfers have known about for a long time – its incredible beaches, crystal clear seas, and waves made for riding.

Mahia Peninsula provides excellent surf no matter from which direction the wind comes. If the wind changes, surfers simply nip across the narrow peninsula to the other shore.

NORTH ISLAND

DID YOU KNOW?

- **The first** of New Zealand's Kerridge chain of cinemas opened in Waipiro Bay. The cinema is now the local marae dining hall.
- **At Tolaga Bay** the southern hemisphere's longest wharf stretches 600 m out to sea. It is a reminder of the region's once thriving farming economy. Local enthusiasts are raising funds for its much needed restoration.
- **An early European historian** once described the Urewera's Tuhoe people as 'children of the mist', thanks to their remote and frequently rain-soaked forest home.
- **The lighthouse** at East Cape used to be located on rugged and hazardous East Island, a few kilometres offshore.
- **The small settlement** of Te Araroa, a few kilometres from East Cape lighthouse, has a 600-year-old pohutukawa tree with over 20 separate trunks.
- **Ruatoria** is the hottest place in the North Island, once reaching a maximum temperature of 39.2°C.
- **Despite** its wonderful climate and scenic attractions the East Cape region remains one of New Zealand's most economically depressed regions. The population is declining and jobs are scarce.
- **Gisborne** was originally known as Turanganui-a-Kiwa, or Turanga for short. Concerned that it might be confused with Tauranga, it was renamed after a local politician, William Gisborne, in 1870.

NORTH ISLAND

Hawke's Bay – Fragile Fruitbowl

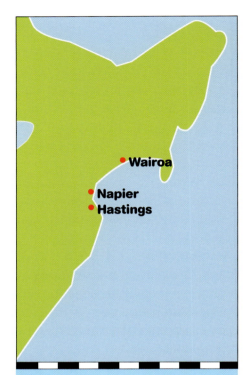

Fertile soils, abundant sunshine and underground water supplies have turned Hawke's Bay's Heretaunga Plains into the country's number one fruit-growing area – New Zealand's 'fruitbowl'. As well as its reputation for pip fruits (apples and pears), stone fruit (peaches and plums) and grapes, many local farms grow vegetables (especially tomatoes, peas, and beans) for processing.

QUICK FACTS:
- The economy is based on farming, forestry and tourism.
- Hastings (population 68,000) and Napier (55,000) are the Bay's main centres.
- Napier is New Zealand's fifth largest port.
- The 1931 Hawke's Bay earthquake killed 256 people.

EVENTS CALENDAR:
February:
Harvest Hawke's Bay – annual wine and food festival
Art Deco Weekend, Napier
International Mission Concert, Napier
April:
Highland Games, Hastings – Scotland in the sun!
September:
Hastings Blossom Festival – springtime celebration
October:
A & P Show – farming spectacular

Horticulture

It wasn't until the 1850s that European farmers took much interest in the Hawke's Bay region, but by the 1930s its fertile Heretaunga Plains had become a horticulturalist's heaven. The well-known New Zealand food processing company, Wattie's, opened its first factory in Hastings in 1934.

French priests were the first to produce wine in Hawke's Bay. Today, Mission Vineyard, New Zealand's oldest vineyard, produces wine for more than strictly religious purposes! There are more than 30 other vineyards in the Hawke's Bay area.

Wattie's has contracts with many local horticulturalists to supply a wide range of fruit and vegetables for processing, canning and freezing.

Shake, rattle and roll

Nature has been kind to Hawke's Bay with its sunny climate and fertile soils, but its underground activities have caused disaster. At 10.47 a.m. on 3 February 1931 a violent earthquake shook Hawke's Bay, killing 256 people. The earthquake raised the bed of the Ahuriri Lagoon stranding boats far from

Cape Kidnappers, at the southern end of Hawke Bay, has one of the world's largest and most accessible mainland gannet colonies.

NORTH ISLAND

DID YOU KNOW?

- **Hawke's Bay** is the name of the region, but the bay is called Hawke Bay.
- **Young gannets** at Cape Kidnappers, like many of their human cousins, shoot off to Australia for a couple of years before returning to New Zealand to settle down and raise a family.
- **Much of old Napier** is on a hill called Scinde Island – well, it was just about an island until the 1931 earthquake surrounded it with land instead of sea.
- **Napier** and Hastings were named after British colonial officials in India. Many streets and local features also have names with Indian associations.
- **Napier** has New Zealand's last remaining marineland. Situated on Marine Parade it holds regular shows of performing dolphins and sealions. Changing attitudes towards keeping wild animals in captivity now prevent the capture of any more dolphins and seals.
- **Napier** holds the North Island record for the most sunshine hours in a year, with 2588 hours in 1994. The average for Napier is 2185 hours, the same as Gisborne but 40 hours less than Tauranga.

the water. Today the 'lagoon' is the site of Napier Airport.

Measuring 7.8 on the Richter scale, the 1931 earthquake destroyed much of Napier and Hastings. In Napier it was fire which completed the devastation. Broken gas lines triggered the fires, and broken water pipes meant they could not be put out. The earthquake still rates as New Zealand's worst ever natural disaster.

Art deco capital of the world

Most of central Napier was rebuilt after the 1931 earthquake in the art deco style of architecture that was popular at the time. Caught in a time warp, Napier has become the art deco capital of the world. People travel from far and wide to walk the 'art deco trails' of this living architectural museum.

Te Mata Peak

According to Maori legend, Te Mata Peak and its jagged ridgeline represents the body of a giant who bit off more than he could chew. Te Mata was set a series of seemingly impossible tasks to win the hand of a local princess. He had achieved all but the final task when he choked on a mountain range he had been instructed to eat. His final bite can still be seen in the mountains behind Havelock North.

Napier's annual Art Deco Weekend is a celebration of the art, architecture and lifestyles of the 1930s.

NORTH ISLAND

Volcanic Plateau – Pumice, Plantations and Power

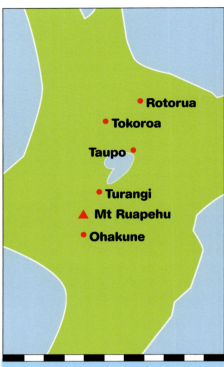

Kaingaroa Forest, once the largest plantation forest in the southern hemisphere, covers a massive 138,000 hectares. Originally owned by the government, much of it was planted by unemployed New Zealanders during the Depression years of the late 1920s and early 1930s.

Forestry

Poor soils delayed the spread of farming into the Volcanic Plateau. By the 1930s a new fertiliser had been developed which made farming possible, but by then vast tracts of the plateau had been planted in exotic pine trees. When the trees matured about 25 years later timber mills were built and a successful new industry was born. The Monterrey Pine grows much more quickly in New Zealand than it does in its native California. Known here as radiata pine it has become the backbone of New Zealand's forest industry.

QUICK FACTS:
- The Volcanic Plateau extends from Mount Ruapehu to the Bay of Plenty.
- It includes the volcanic centres of Okataina (Rotorua), Taupo and Tongariro.
- The economy is based on forestry, hydroelectric power generation and tourism.
- The main centres are Taupo, Rotorua, Turangi and Tokoroa.

EVENTS CALENDAR:
November:
Golden Axe Carnival, Tokoroa

The Forestry Cycle

- Seedlings are grown in a nursery.
- Seedlings are planted out on cleared land.
- Young trees are pruned as branches cause knots in the timber.
- Trees are thinned to allow room for growth.
- After about 25-30 years the trees are felled.
- Powerful logging trucks take the logs to the mill.
- Logs are processed into timber and wood products.

Thousands of years ago eruptions of the Taupo volcano spread ash and pumice over much of the Volcanic Plateau. The soils that developed on these volcanic deposits lacked the mineral cobalt. When pastures for sheep and cattle farming were grown on these soils the animals developed 'bush sickness'.

NORTH ISLAND

DID YOU KNOW?

- **The Tongariro Hydroelectric Power Scheme** carefully avoids the Whangaehu River. Flowing from Ruapehu's crater lake its water is too acidic to take through the expensive turbines in the power stations.
- **The Wairakei power station** was the world's second large-scale geothermal power station. The first was in Italy.
- **In the right weather conditions**, clouds of steam released from the Wairakei geothermal power station can create a road hazard – poor visibility.
- **Many homes in Rotorua** had their geothermal bores disconnected when it was feared they were causing the famous Pohutu geyser at the nearby Whakarewarewa Thermal Reserve to lose its power.
- **Kaingaroa Forest** is the world's largest radiata pine plantation.

Forestry

The Kinleith Pulp and Paper Mill was built in the 1950s to process logs from the maturing pine forests. The planned township of Tokoroa grew rapidly to house the forestry and mill workers, many of whom were Maori and Pacific Islanders, attracted from economically depressed areas of New Zealand and the Pacific.

New Zealand's pine forests provide for its construction timber needs and much of its paper requirements. Over one million tonnes of pulp and paper and about seven million cubic metres of timber are exported annually, earning New Zealand about 2.5 billion dollars a year; 75 per cent of these exports go to Japan, Australia and Korea.

Hydro power

Many of the rivers and streams flowing from the mountains of Tongariro National Park have been 'captured' for hydroelectric power generation. The Tongariro Hydroelectric Power Scheme required complex diversions of rivers, and specialist tunnelling expertise was imported from Italy. The town of Turangi was built in 1964 to house the scheme's labour force. The power scheme was completed in the 1980s and Turangi is now primarily a tourist centre.

The Tongariro Hydroelectric Power Scheme involves the complex diversion of streams through a series of tunnels and lakes to supply the Rangipo and Tokaanu power stations.

Geothermal power

Maori have lived with the Volcanic Plateau's geothermal resources for hundreds of years, using hot springs for cooking, washing and heating. In 1963 a geo-thermal power station started generating electricity at Wairakei, and a second was commissioned at Ohaaki in 1989. These power stations use naturally produced steam to turn turbines and generate electricity.

Tourism

The Volcanic Plateau is the North Island's most important tourist destination. From Rotorua in the north to Mount Ruapehu in the south, its spectacular natural and cultural attractions draw tourists all year round. Tongariro National Park offers winter skiing and summer walks. Lake Taupo and the streams flowing into it are renowned for their trout fishing and Rotorua offers a unique blend of Maori culture and geothermal wonders. (See pages 34-35.)

The natural steam taken from the ground is too wet and has to have its water content removed. 'Dry' steam is then piped to the power station where it turns turbines and generates electricity.

NORTH ISLAND

Volcanic Plateau – Rotorua and Taupo

Rotorua is the heart of Maori tourism. Here more than anywhere else in New Zealand tourists are offered experiences about Maori by Maori. These include an evening concert of song and dance in a carved meeting house, a hangi meal cooked in a traditional earth oven, and an overnight stay at local marae.

QUICK FACTS:

- Rotorua was New Zealand's first major tourist resort.
- Rotorua's permanent population is 57,000.
- Taupo's permanent population is 18,000.

EVENTS CALENDAR:

March:
Ironman New Zealand – cycle, swim and run round Lake Taupo
April:
Lake Taupo International Trout Fishing Tournament
May:
Rotorua Marathon
November:
Rotorua International Trout Tournament
December:
Lake Taupo Power Boat Race

Rotorua

Rotorua is New Zealand's oldest tourist resort. It offers visitors a unique combination of natural wonders and cultural experiences.

It is not only a great honour but also a great responsibility for promising carvers from around the country to be selected for training at Rotorua's Maori Arts and Crafts Institute.

A violent volcanic past

Rotorua sits rather precariously at the northern end of the Taupo volcanic zone. The most recent eruption was in 1886 when Mount Tarawera blew its top, killing 150 people. To the visitor, Rotorua's most obvious connection with the 'fire in its belly' is the unavoidable and sulphurous smell of geothermal activity.

Rotorua's geysers, like Pohutu, are as spectacular as they are unreliable for the camera-clicking! The Whakarewarewa Thermal Reserve is owned, operated and lived in by local Maori. Its geothermal resources provide hot water for cooking, washing and heating as well as an income from inquisitive tourists.

When Tarawera burst into life in 1886 it caused the death of 150 people. Most of the deaths were caused when ash and mud completely buried three Maori villages close to the mountain.

Te Wairoa is now promoted as a 'buried village' tourist attraction.

Lake Rotorua is a caldera – the collapsed crater of a large volcano. Mokoia Island indicates its central vent. Local legends tell the story of the beautiful Hinemoa and her courageous swim to Mokoia Island to be with her lover, Tutanekai. Today, the lake offers superb trout fishing, and fishing guides virtually guarantee tourists a catch.

Thrills and spills

Rotorua, like most tourist centres in New Zealand, offers adrenalin-pumping activities. In recent years a range of adventure activities such as white-water rafting, four-wheel-drive safaris and sky-diving have been added to Rotorua's tourist 'menu'.

Taupo

Taupo is less than two hours' drive from Rotorua. Like Rotorua, it is situated on the shores of a volcanic lake, has geothermal activity, and offers outstanding fishing and adventure tourism thrills. It does not offer Rotorua's Maori cultural experiences, but it is within striking distance of Tongariro National Park.

Lake Taupo dwarfs the neighbouring volcanoes of Ruapehu, Tongariro and Ngauruhoe. Taupo's eruptions of 30,000 and 1800 years ago were some of the world's largest. They covered most of the North Island in ash and left behind a huge caldera that has since filled with water to form Lake Taupo.

To an angler, Turangi, Taupo and Tongariro mean one thing – trout! The lake and its in-flowing rivers offer some of the best trout fishing in the world. Brown trout were introduced to New Zealand from Tasmania in 1868. Rainbow trout followed in 1882 from California.

The National Trout Centre on the banks of the Tongariro River is one of only three hatcheries in New Zealand. Its rainbow trout are released into rivers and lakes throughout the country when they are year-old fingerlings. Trout ova (eggs) are even sent overseas.

Postcard from Rotorua

Kia ora!

I've hongi-ed and hangi-ed my way through this amazing place! I've even got used to the smell — real bad-eggs stuff. Waited for ages to get one half-decent photo of Pohutu geyser at Whaka-what's-it-called, and then took about fifty in no time at Lady Knox.

Nearly bought a sheep at a farm show, but it wouldn't fit into my bag, even after it had been shorn! You should have seen the way the sheep dogs dealt with the stroppy sheep. We could do with some of the noisy huntaway dogs for the football crowds at home.

Off to Taupo tomorrow — if Tarawera doesn't blow its top again! We're taking the 4WD safari up to the Tarawera crater in the morning.

Ka kite! (Geez, I'm picking up the lingo quickly!)
Pete

Matthew Smith
79 Jones Rd
Palmerston North

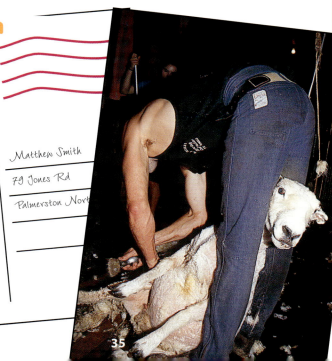

With the help of a skilled shearer, New Zealand sheep can get undressed in less than a minute. Ewe'd be amazed!

NORTH ISLAND

DID YOU KNOW?

- **Taupo's** rainbow trout are considered to be some of the most genetically pure in the world. Their eggs are exported for trout breeding programmes in many countries.
- **The quality** of Lake Taupo's clear, blue water is being threatened by the development of dairy farming, housing and forestry around its shores.
- **Along the eastern shore** of Lake Taupo swimmers can be pleasantly surprised by areas of warm water. Hot springs near the shoreline act like hidden hot taps!
- **Taupo** is short for Taupo-nui-a-Tia, meaning 'the great flax cape of Tia'. Tia is said to have come to New Zealand on the Arawa canoe.
- **In 1881** modern Rotorua was developed by the government as a 'spa' town, where people could cure their aches and pains in its thermal waters and mud. Its first building was a bath-house! Its hospital still specialises in the treatment of rheumatism.
- **The Lady Knox Geyser**, at Waiotapu between Rotorua and Taupo, performs spectacularly at precisely the same time every day for hundreds of admiring tourists. The trick of putting soap in it was discovered around 1900 by prisoners washing their clothes.
- **Rotorua** means 'second lake'. Presumably neighbouring, but smaller, Rotoiti is the first lake. The town took its name from the lake, rather than the existing village of Ohinemutu.
- **The eruption** of Tarawera in 1886 destroyed Rotorua's main tourist attraction, the Pink and White Terraces. This spectacular series of silica-fringed pools was once considered one of the world's natural wonders.

NORTH ISLAND

Tongariro National Park – Gift to the Nation

Ngauruhoe, the second highest mountain in the Park, last erupted lava in 1954. Between 1939 and 1975 it erupted over 60 times, making it New Zealand's most active volcano. It has been relatively quiet since then.

According to Maori legend Tongariro's volcanic fire was sent from Hawaiki, their Pacific homeland. When Ngatoro-i-rangi, a Tuwharetoa priest, climbed high into Tongariro's mountains he was chilled by a snowstorm. His desperate call to his sisters in Hawaiki for fire to warm him was answered by a volcanic eruption.

In 1887, Tuwharetoa chief Te Heuheu Tukino IV offered the mountains of Ruapehu, Ngauruhoe and Tongariro to the government on the condition that they be set aside as a reserve for the whole country, a national park. The government accepted the gift and Tongariro National Park was established in 1894.

Scientific theory links Tongariro's volcanic activity with New Zealand's Pacific Island neighbours. The 'Pacific Ring of Fire' represents a line of earthquake and volcanic activity around the perimeter of the enormous Pacific Plate. Alongside the North Island of New Zealand the Pacific Plate plunges beneath the Australian Plate, stirring up a fiery mix of magma, rock and mud. Every so often this mix erupts on to the surface as lava and ash.

In 1995 and 1996 Mount Ruapehu burst into life again, reminding New Zealanders that Tongariro National Park is an active volcanic zone. The Park's dramatic volcanic landscapes and varied vegetation attract hikers from around New Zealand and the world.

QUICK FACTS:
- Tongariro National Park, established in 1894, was New Zealand's first national park.
- Highest mountains: Ruapehu (2797 m), Ngauruhoe (2291 m), Tongariro (1968 m)
- The park covers 75,500 hectares.
- There are large commercial skifields at Whakapapa and Turoa.

EVENTS CALENDAR:
July: Ski season opens
October: Ski season closes
December: National Park Summer Visitor Programme begins

In 1991 it was listed as a World Heritage site for its natural and cultural significance.

Tongariro: Although it gives its name to the Park, it is only the Park's third highest mountain. Ketetahi Springs, Red Crater and the Emerald Lakes are admired by trampers on the popular Tongariro crossing walk.

Crater Lake: Ruapehu's fascinating crater lake rises and falls according to levels of volcanic activity. In 1953 an ice wall gave way and the lake's water flooded the Whangaehu valley. Over 30 kilometres downstream the Tangiwai rail bridge was washed away only minutes before the Wellington-Auckland train arrived. The first six carriages were lost in the flood and 151 people died.

Taranaki Falls: Melting snows and solidified flows of lava combine to create spectacular waterfalls on Ruapehu's slopes.

Rangipo Desert: The pumice slopes of Ruapehu's more sheltered, eastern side give them a stark, desert-like appearance. The lower, more exposed, southwestern slopes are draped with dense beech forests.

Winter wonderland

Although Ruapehu's summit has permanent snow and several small glaciers, heavy snowfalls between July and October transform it into a winter playground. Skiers, mainly from the North Island and Australia, flock to its two commercial skifields at Whakapapa and Turoa.

Skiing the 'magic mountain' on Whakapapa's well-groomed slopes.

Every so often Ruapehu coughs and splutters, rudely interrupting the business of skiing. The eruptions of 1995 and 1996 closed the mountain's skifields and cost the local ski industry millions of dollars in lost income.

Ohakune, a once sleepy rural town, better known for its fields of carrots, is now a vibrant all-year resort, offering winter snow sports and summer walking, rafting and horse riding.

Railway feats

The early tourist development of Tongariro National Park was boosted by the completion of the North Island's Main Trunk railway line in 1908. Spectacular feats of engineering were needed to get the line up to stations at National Park and Ohakune, such as the famous Raurimu Spiral. By looping back on itself

NORTH ISLAND

DID YOU KNOW?

- **Ngauruhoe** is a fine example of a strato volcano, built up by alternating layers of ash and lava.
- **Ruapehu** was first climbed by Europeans in 1879. Skiing began on its slopes in 1913.
- **At birth**, Tuwharetoa chief Te Heuheu Tukino IV was named 'Horonuku' (landslide), in memory of his grandfather who had been killed by a landslide.
- **Tuwharetoa's** original gift of about 2600 hectares around the three volcanoes has been added to by the government over the years. The Park now covers 75,500 hectares.
- **Yellowstone National Park**, USA, became the world's first national park in 1872. Tongariro was the second.
- **The Chateau**, New Zealand's highest hotel, was built in 1929 at an altitude of 1127 m. From 1942 to 1945 it was used as a mental hospital.
- **The Park** environment is fragile and needs careful management. Exotic pine trees, spread by wind from plantations outside the national park, are likely to change the Park's character unless eradication programmes are successful.
- **Ruapehu's** eruptions in 1995 and 1996 were estimated to have cost over $140 million.

at Raurimu, the Main Trunk railway line reduces its gradient to a manageable 1:50 as it ascends the steep lower slopes of Mount Ruapehu.

Makatote Viaduct: Spectacular viaducts carry the Main Trunk line across the deep chasms of Ruapehu's western slopes.

NORTH ISLAND

Taranaki – From the Mountain to the Sea

Maori legend tells how Taranaki once stood alongside Ruapehu in the centre of the North Island. Unable to win the love of beautiful Pihanga, the gentle mountain on the southern shores of Lake Taupo, Taranaki fled to the west coast. The valley of the Whanganui River traces his journey.

Mount Taranaki dominates the province that shares its name. It has seen some dramatic changes since the 1860s as Taranaki has moved from war to peace and from forest to pasture and petroleum.

Now a peaceful town, Waitara is where the Taranaki Land Wars began. In 1860 Wiremu Kingi challenged an illegal sale of land to the government which responded by sending in troops and confiscating virtually the whole Taranaki Province. Heavily out-numbered by government troops, Taranaki Maori fought a guerrilla-style war which continued, on and off, for the next 21 years.

In 1865 Maori prophets Te Whiti and Tohu withdrew with their many followers to Parihaka. They advocated non-violent resistance to Pakeha invasion. After ploughing up settlers' paddocks, pulling out surveyors' pegs and erecting fences across roads, Te Whiti's followers did not resist arrest. There were always more volunteers and soon the jails were overflowing.

In 1881 the government lost patience and, to its shame, sent troops into Parihaka. Once again they met no resistance, only hospitality, before arresting and jailing Te Whiti and Tohu. Never brought to trial, the prophets were released in 1883. Te Whiti remained at Parihaka until his death in 1907. Te Whiti's pacifist opposition to oppression has since been compared to Mahatma Gandhi's non-violent campaigns against the British in India some years later.

From peace to pasture and Park
After peace was finally made in 1881, Pakeha settlers soon cleared the forests and established dairy farms on Taranaki's lower slopes. Fertile soils, plenty of rain and mild temperatures

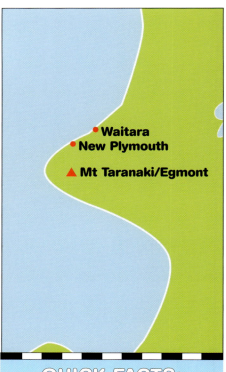

QUICK FACTS:
- Mount Taranaki, a dormant volcano, rises 2518 m above sea level.
- New Plymouth (population 49,000) is Taranaki's main urban centre.
- The economy is dominated by dairy farming and the oil and gas industry.

EVENTS CALENDAR:
February:
Hawera Dairy Festival
March:
Mountain to Surf Marathon
October:
Rhododendron Festival

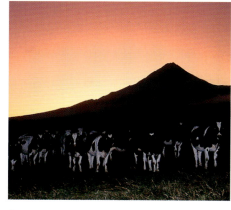

Taranaki remains one of New Zealand's main dairying regions today and accounts for about 15 per cent of New Zealand's total dairy herd.

Taranaki's 2158 m peak brings snow and skiers to its slopes. It could also bring serious trouble. Volcanic activity is carefully monitored and early warning systems should allow time for evacuation – not only of the skifields but also any farms and towns threatened by lahars.

soon made Taranaki the most important dairying region in New Zealand. The upper slopes of the mountain were saved from the axe and saw to prevent flooding on the surrounding farms. In 1900 Egmont National Park was created.

Oil and gas

Taranaki is the home of New Zealand's oil and gas industry. Its eight oil and gas fields produce about one third of New Zealand's oil needs. About half its gas is used to make methanol and synthetic petrol at Waitara and Motonui; a quarter generates electricity and the rest is supplied to industry and homes.

Volcanic hazards

Although Egmont National Park's forests provide some protection against floods, they could not hold back fast-moving volcanic mudflows (lahars). Taranaki has not erupted since about 1660, but future eruptions are possible.

NORTH ISLAND

DID YOU KNOW?

- **In 1770** Captain Cook and his crew were the first Europeans to see the summit of Taranaki. It had been covered in cloud when Abel Tasman sailed by in 1642.
- **When Captain Cook** spotted Taranaki in 1770 he named it 'Egmont' after his boss (First Lord of the Admiralty) Lord Egmont. Over two hundred years later, its original name was restored by New Zealand's Geographic Board. It is now officially known as Mount Taranaki/Egmont. The national park, a nearby cape and the mountain village all retained the name of Egmont.
- **The British Empire's** first oil strike was at Motuora, New Plymouth, in 1865. Nearly a century passed, however, before Taranaki's oil and gas fields were developed commercially.
- **Passing Japanese fishermen** have been known to pray to Taranaki. It has a striking similarity to sacred Mount Fuji in Japan.
- **Taranaki dairy farms** are the home of the simple but effective 'Taranaki gate'.
- **A Taranaki dairy factory** supplies mozzarella cheese for Pizza Huts around the world!

Two-thirds of New Zealand's gas reserves and half of its oil reserves lie deep below the sea in the offshore Maui field. The onshore Kapuni field is the second largest.

NORTH ISLAND

Whanganui and Manawatu – From River to Plain

The Whanganui River is now a popular destination for those looking for all kinds of water sports.

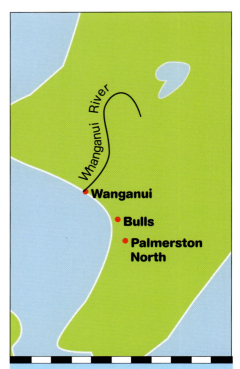

QUICK FACTS:

- The Whanganui River (290 km) is New Zealand's third longest river.
- Wanganui (population 41,000) lies at the mouth of the Whanganui River.
- Palmerston North (population 74,000) is one of New Zealand's few inland cities.
- The Manawatu Plains are an important agricultural area.

EVENTS CALENDAR:

February:
New Zealand Masters' Games, Wanganui (every odd-numbered year)
October:
Mountains to the Sea Triathlon (Ruapehu to Wanganui)
November:
Wanganui Festival and A & P Show

The scenic, cultural and historical significance of the Whanganui River was recognised by the creation of the Whanganui National Park in 1986. It is New Zealand's third longest river, and its most navigable. After tumbling steeply off the western slopes of Mount Ruapehu it flows first north and then south through steep and easily eroded hill country before lazily winding its way to the sea at Wanganui.

History

The Whanganui River, teeming with eels, was a rich source of food for Maori. Thousands of slippery eels were caught at a time in huge traps set across the river.

To the Maori the Whanganui River had been a canoe 'highway', long before the arrival of Europeans. The river extends almost to Lake Taupo, which gave access to the Waikato River system and the top of the North Island. In the nineteenth century the Whanganui became a vital transport route for Europeans as well.

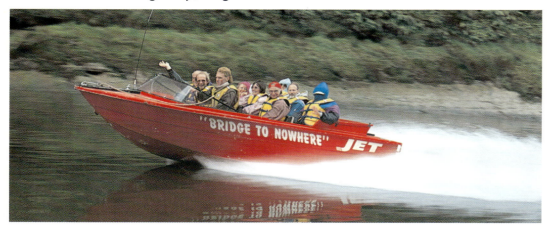

Whanganui National Park

Whanganui National Park does not actually include the Whanganui River.

The river remains in Maori ownership, but without it there wouldn't be a national park! The best way to approach the park is from the river, either by jet boat, canoe or kayak.

Wanganui

Wanganui was established as a European settlement in 1840, but the way the land was acquired from local Maori still causes resentment and protest today. Wanganui was well situated at the mouth of an important river. It grew rapidly through the nineteenth century but lost much of its earlier strategic importance when the Main Trunk railway line was completed in 1908.

Bypassed by major road and rail links, Wanganui now serves its local hinterland. Meat and wool from the hilly interior and the fertile coastal plains are processed in Wanganui; and it does keep an eye on what the rest of the country gets up to – it is the home of the National Police Computer.

Manawatu Plains

The coastal plains and downlands of the Manawatu contrast strongly with the hills and gorges of the Whanganui. The fertile plains are an important livestock farming and cereal-growing region.

A Manawatu mixed farm grows crops and grazes livestock in a regular rotation to help preserve the soil's natural fertility. The Manawatu Plains are the North Island's answer to the Canterbury Plains of the South Island.

Palmerston North is the main centre of this productive agricultural region. It benefited as much as Wanganui suffered when it was connected to the Main Trunk railway line. Palmerston North, home of Massey University, is also an important education and agricultural research centre.

International Pacific College.

The 'Bridge to Nowhere' tells the story of failed attempts to clear, farm and settle rugged hill country near Pipiriki at the end of the First World War. Hard to get to and hampered by soil erosion and regenerating bush, the land had been abandoned by pioneer settlers by 1942. Only the bridge – to nowhere – remains.

NORTH ISLAND

DID YOU KNOW?

- **Somewhere** along the way Wanganui lost its 'h'! It has now been given back to the river and the national park, but the town is still officially Wanganui, not Whanganui.
- **A monument** in Wanganui's Moutua Gardens remembers local Maori who, in 1864, were killed defending the European settlement from rival Maori attack.
- **In 1864** Wanganui was being considered as a possible site for New Zealand's capital. It lost out to Wellington.
- **In 1962** Peter Snell set a world record for the mile running on grass at Wanganui's Cook's Gardens.
- **A Wanganui chief** received a blanket for signing the Treaty of Waitangi in 1840 – he thought he was signing a receipt for a blanket sent to him by Queen Victoria! No wonder there have been arguments about the Treaty.
- **Palmerston North** was known as Palmerston until 1873. There were several other Palmerstons in New Zealand at the time. Many new names were considered before the townspeople reached an unhappy compromise. They simply stuck a 'North' on the end!
- **An estimated** 40 per cent of Palmerston North's population is in some way involved with higher education, giving it the nickname of 'Knowledge City'.
- **You can get milk** from bulls! It's possible in a small rural town between Wanganui and Palmerston North – you just walk into a dairy and buy it. By the way, the town is called Bulls.

NORTH ISLAND

Wellington – Capital City

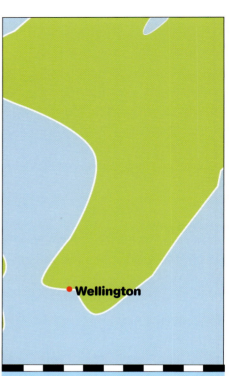

QUICK FACTS:
- Wellington was New Zealand's first organised European settlement.
- Wellington has been capital since 1865.
- Wellington (population 335,000) is New Zealand's second largest city.
- Te Papa, New Zealand's national museum, is in Wellington.

EVENTS CALENDAR:
January:
Wellington Anniversary Day
February:
Opening of Parliament
International Festival of the Arts
(every two years)
July:
Wellington Film Festival

In 1865 New Zealand's capital moved south for the second time and came to Wellington. The majority of European settlers lived in the South Island and Wellington was a more central location.
If the capital had not come to Wellington, and gone instead to Wanganui or Nelson, then Wellington today may be no larger than Picton, at the other end of the Cook Strait ferry crossing.

Parliament

Every three years New Zealanders elect their political representatives. These members of Parliament (MPs) meet in Wellington to debate the important issues of the day and pass legislation. The political party with the most MPs usually forms the government. This may be done by two or more parties joining together in a coalition, with the leader of the largest party usually becoming the prime minister. New Zealand's parliamentary system of government has evolved from the British system introduced in the nineteenth century.

The main Parliament Building, where 120 MPs debate the issues of government, was built in 1922 out of Takaka marble.

Vogel House is the prime minister's official residence in Wellington.
In 1840 the Treaty of Waitangi established Britain's Queen Victoria as queen of New Zealand. Today, a British queen still 'rules' over New Zealand. Her representative, the Governor-General, lives at Government House in Wellington.

Government Buildings: This imitation stone building, built in 1876 to accommodate government bureaucrats, is actually one of the largest wooden buildings in the world. It is now used by Victoria University.

Wellington's Beehive is the most recognisable of its buildings. Built in 1981, it provides offices for the nation's politicians. Parliament meets in the older building next door.

NORTH ISLAND

DID YOU KNOW?

- **The New Zealand Company** originally placed its settlers at Britannia (in the Hutt Valley) on the other side of the harbour. Hit by floods, the young settlement was moved to Lambton Harbour in 1840 and renamed Wellington, in honour of Britain's Duke of Wellington.
- **Katherine Mansfield**, one of New Zealand's greatest novelists, was born in Wellington in 1888. Her birthplace has been restored and is open to visitors.
- **When New Zealand** changed its system of government in 1996 it increased the number of MPs to 120. Extra office space was provided in a building over the road and an underground tunnel gives them quick access to the debating chamber.
- **There are very few roads** out of central Wellington. It could easily be cut off by an earthquake or landslip.
- **The beach** at Wellington's inner-city Oriental Bay isn't a natural beach at all. Its sands came from the ballast of nineteeth century British sailing ships.

Cultural capital

Wellington's capital status has given it a distinctive character. As well as all its politicians, government officials and public servants, the capital attracts foreign diplomats and the head office staff of major companies and organisations. They all want to be close to the 'seat of power'. Well educated and well paid, they support a wide range of theatres, museums, libraries and art galleries in Wellington.

Te Papa Tongarewa

The National Museum of New Zealand is an interactive museum of the future. Completed in 1998, it completely revolutionised New Zealanders' views of what museums should be like. It received two million visitors in its first year.

The National Archives

Our nation's cultural treasure trove preserves priceless items from New Zealand's past. The original Treaty of Waitangi document is kept here.

Regional stadium

Wellington's new multi-sport regional stadium was opened at the start of a new millennium. It is situated on reclaimed land by the railway station.

'Absolutely positive'

Wellington architects have a habit of designing striking buildings. Maybe it is something to do with the city's dramatic setting and startling views, or is it the brooding threat of a major earthquake (see pages 44-45)? Whatever it is, Wellingtonians are 'absolutely positive' about their city and this attitude is reflected in its architecture.

NORTH ISLAND

Wellington – Facing the Elements

Wellington, hanging on to the southern tip of the North Island, is challenged by winds, threatened by earthquakes and inspired by views. Wellingtonians are always facing the elements!

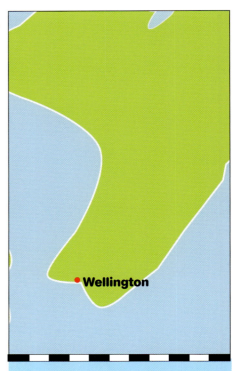

QUICK FACTS:
- Three active fault lines run through Wellington.
- Wellington's last major earthquake was in 1855.
- Much of downtown Wellington is built on reclaimed land.

Had New Zealand's capital moved south in 1855 rather than 1865 it may have kept on moving. 1855 was the year of the Wairarapa earthquake. It gave the small settlement of Wellington a severe shaking and changed its shoreline considerably. Some recent arrivals packed their bags and headed back to England on the next ship! Politicians may not have been too impressed, either.

The Wairarapa earthquake, whose epicentre was only 20 km from central Wellington, is the largest to have struck New Zealand since European settlement began. It is estimated to have measured a massive 8.2 on the Richter scale. Few were living in Wellington at the time and only five people were killed, but it has had a lasting effect on the city.

Wellington's Basin Reserve, now a well-known cricket ground, was originally planned as a 'basin' for ships: it was to be linked by canal to the harbour. These plans changed after the 1855 Wairarapa earthquake raised Wellington by about 1.5 metres, stranding the basin high and dry!

The 1855 Wairarapa earthquake exposed land at the foot of the cliffs along the western shores of the harbour. It was along this raised beach that the Hutt Valley motorway and railway line were built.

Waiting for 'the big one'!
Greater Wellington sits across three active faultlines. The Wellington Fault runs right through the centre of the city, and no new buildings are allowed to be built over it. Only 20 km to the east lies the West Wairarapa Fault, which caused

the 1855 Wairarapa earthquake. Wellington is definitely earthquake territory and another large earthquake is expected – some time!

When Parliament Buildings were renovated (1992-95) they had special 'shock absorbers' fitted to their foundations. This earthquake-proofing technique, called base isolation, was invented by New Zealander Bill Robinson. It has already proved its effectiveness in earthquakes in New Zealand and overseas. This must be reassuring to our MPs as they debate important issues only 400 m from the Wellington Fault.

NORTH ISLAND

DID YOU KNOW?
- **Windy Wellington** has more calm days than Auckland. It also has many more very windy days!
- **The 1855** Wairarapa earthquake left Wellington's jetties stranded out of the water.
- **A major earthquake** near Wellington could cause large waves – called seiches – to bounce back and forth across the harbour several times.

the inter-island ferry was blown onto rocks at the mouth of Wellington harbour. The ship capsized and 51 lives were lost.

High above the city an experimental wind turbine makes the most of Wellington's windy reputation.

Wind-generated electricity may one day supply much of Wellington's power needs.

Mount Victoria provides spectacular views of Wellington's harbour and city.

Reclamation and elevation

The Wairarapa earthquake increased the amount of flat land around Wellington's shoreline. Rapid population growth after it became capital in 1865 resulted in more land being reclaimed from the sea. About one fifth of central Wellington is now built on reclaimed land.

Hemmed in by steep hills, most of Wellington's business district is built on land reclaimed from the sea. Streets like Lambton Quay and Thorndon Quay, where ships once docked, mark the artificial progression of the shoreline.

With little flat land available for housing, Wellington's suburbs took to the steep hillsides around its harbour. Wellington is renowned for its steep, zig-zagging roads, footpaths and steps. Most famous of all is the cable car that connects the heart of the city to the suburban heights of Kelburn.

Windy Wellington

Winds whistling through the narrows of Cook Strait are responsible for Wellington's windy reputation. Wellingtonians sometimes make good use of their wind, but usually when the biting southerlies blow in they just grin and bare as little as possible. On 10 April 1968, however, the winds caused the *Wahine* disaster.

Battered by winds gusting up to 148 kph

April 10th, 1968. 51 die in Wahine Disaster.
Had this ship been nuclear powered, thousands could have died.

Viewpoints

Living high on the city's hills not only offers residents plenty of wind, it also gives them stunning views.

SOUTH ISLAND

Top of the South – Sunny Marlborough and Nelson

Picton is best known for its end-of-the-railway-line ferry terminal. Several times each day ferries sail across Cook Strait linking Wellington and Picton. The proposed new ferry terminal at Clifford Bay, south of Blenheim, would divert most Cook Strait traffic away from Picton and have a major impact on its economy.

The Nelson and Marlborough districts at the 'top of the south' are New Zealand's sunniest places. Their fertile plains, sheltered from wind and rain by mountains, produce some of New Zealand's best horticultural crops. Forestry has been developed on less fertile surrounding hill country.

Marlborough's first vines were established as recently as the 1970s. Only 25 years later it had become New Zealand's leading wine-producing district, an achievement celebrated each year at the Marlborough Wine and Food Festival.

Apples, pears, kiwifruit and a variety of stone and berry fruits grow in abundance along Nelson's fruit belt between Richmond and Motueka. Large quantities of tobacco were once grown here. Hops, for beer making, still are.

Riches from the sea
Nelson and Marlborough make a living from the sea as well as the sun and soil. With easy access to all coasts, Port Nelson is the centre of New Zealand's fishing industry.

More than half New Zealand's total fishing catch is taken by 20 seafood companies based in Nelson, the 'seafood capital of New Zealand'. Mussel farms also abound in the sheltered waters of the Marlborough Sounds and Golden Bay. At Lake Grasmere, sun and sea combine to produce salt from ponds of sea water.

QUICK FACTS:
- Blenheim is New Zealand's sunniest place, averaging 2470 sunshine hours a year.
- Nelson holds the New Zealand annual sunshine record with 2711 hours in 1931.
- Marlborough suffers periodically from drought.
- Nelson (population 52,000) has twice the number of people as Blenheim (26,000).
- The economy of the Nelson-Marlborough region is based on horticulture, fishing, forestry and tourism.

EVENTS CALENDAR:
February:
Nelson's Anniversary Day
Marlborough Wine and Food Festival
April:
Packers and Pickers Ball –
a kind of harvest festival
July:
Golden Bay Scallop Festival
September:
New Zealand Wearable Art Awards
November:
Garden Marlborough Wine and Gardening Festival
December:
Havelock Mussel Festival

Tourism

Natural attractions of land, lake and sea attract thousands of tourists each year from New Zealand and around the world.

Kahurangi National Park is the most recent and second largest of New Zealand's national parks. Walking the Heaphy Track is a popular way to experience the Park's wide variety of landscapes. It contains over half of New Zealand's native plant species.

Abel Tasman National Park is New Zealand's smallest national park but arguably its most beautiful. Its coastal walk follows a succession of sparkling blue bays, golden beaches, rocky headlands and dense bush.

Nelson Lakes National Park offers a range of outdoor activities from boating and fishing on its lakes to walking, climbing, skiing and hunting in its rugged high country. The Park is named after Lake Rotoiti and Lake Rotoroa (not to be confused with lakes of the same name in Rotorua). Park administration and accommodation is based at St Arnaud.

Marlborough Sounds Maritime Park provides welcome relief to passengers crossing from Wellington on the Cook Strait ferry. Its calm waters and fingerlike headlands are the result of a 'drowned' landscape. 'The Sounds' are a popular holiday retreat for 'boaties' and those wanting to get away from it all.

Kaikoura Kaikoura means 'eating crayfish', but to tourists it means whales! In the past whales were hunted and killed here. Today's whaling industry is based on protecting and watching them. Dolphins and seals provide popular sideshows for tourists.

History

Maori ownership of the top of the South Island was hotly contested. The area had been ravaged by tribal wars and was not heavily populated when European settlement began in the 1840s.

Golden Bay When Abel Tasman sailed into what is now called Golden Bay in 1642, four of his crew were killed by Maori. He left in a hurry, without having set foot on New Zealand, naming the place Murderers Bay. It became Coal Bay after the discovery of coal at Takaka 1842, and finally Golden Bay after the discovery of gold in 1857.

Nelson was established in 1842 on land bought from Te Rauparaha by the New Zealand Company in the same year. In 1858 it became New Zealand's first official 'city', not because of its size but because of its bishop! In 1865 it missed out on becoming the nation's new capital. Wellington was chosen instead.

SOUTH ISLAND

DID YOU KNOW?

- **Nelson** is slightly further north than Wellington. Cape Farewell, at the top of the South Island, is nearly as far north as Palmerston North.
- **Sheep** were first introduced into the South Island through the port of Picton.
- **Farewell Spit** (35 km) is New Zealand's longest spit.
- **Nettlebed Cave**, northwest Nelson, is New Zealand's deepest cave (899 m).
- **The first game of rugby** ever played in New Zealand took place in Nelson in 1870. Nelson Football Club beat Nelson College 2-0. Goals, not tries, were what mattered.
- **The Marlborough Sounds** are so 'wrinkled' that Pelorus Sound, which is only 45 km from end to end, has a 380 km shoreline!
- **Nelson** was named after British naval hero Horatio Nelson.
- **Blenheim** was originally called Beavertown because of its situation next to a flood-prone river.
- **Although Nelson** does not have a university it has long attracted well-educated and creative people. It offers a wide range of cultural activities, including the annual 'Wearable Art Awards'.

Blenheim became established after land in the Wairau Valley was purchased by the government in 1847. An earlier attempt by European settlers to claim the land in 1843 was resisted by Ngati Toa and their chief, Te Rauparaha. Eight Maori and 22 Europeans were killed in what proved to be the last armed conflict between Maori and European in the south.

SOUTH ISLAND

West Coast – Extraction v Conservation

In this picture postcard scene New Zealand's highest mountains are mirrored in the still waters of Lake Matheson. The West Coast's mountains and forests were once considered barriers to the region's development. They are now its main attraction.

QUICK FACTS:
- The West Coast's population has been declining since the 1960s.
- Its main towns are Westport, Greymouth and Hokitika.
- The climate is cool and very wet (4000-13,000 mm of rain per year).
- The economy is based on tourism, mining and forestry.

EVENTS CALENDAR:
February:
Buller Gorge Marathon
March:
Wild Foods Festival, Hokitika
September:
Whitebait season begins on Buller River

New Zealand's West Coast is rich in natural resources. It has some of the country's most spectacular mountains, forests and rivers, which contain some of the country's most valuable industrial raw materials. Over 30,000 people live on 'the Coast', and a battle rages about how the 'Coasters' should earn a living. In the past they worked as miners, loggers and sawmillers, extracting the gold, coal and timber. The future, how-ever, may be based more on conservation and protecting the forests, rivers and mountains for a tourist industry.

A tradition of extraction

Greenstone: Greenstone, known to Maori as pounamu, is found among the boulders of West Coast rivers. When West Coast Maori sold most of the West Coast to the government in 1857 they excluded their main greenstone sources from the sale. Pounamu was not only attractive, it was also a very effective cutting tool. It was traded by Maori throughout New Zealand. The South Island became known as Te Wai Pounamu. With limited technology Maori extraction of greenstone had little effect on the environment. The extraction of greenstone is strictly controlled today.

Gold: Gold was found on the West Coast in 1863. Frantic gold rushes over the next four years brought

over 10 per cent of New Zealand's European population to the West Coast. Hokitika became the busiest port in the country. Most of the gold extracted in the 1860s was alluvial gold, taken from the sands and gravels of its rivers. Panning and sluicing later gave way to large scale dredging of the river beds. In the 1870s 'quartz gold' was mined near Reefton. By 1895 gold mining was declining on the West Coast and people either moved away or turned to farming, logging or coal mining. By the 1990s new mining technology had renewed gold mining interest on the West Coast. There's still plenty of gold on the Coast.

Coal: Coal mining replaced gold mining as the Coast's main industry by 1900. The Grey (near Greymouth) and Buller (near Westport) coalfields were the most important. Coal mining dominated the Coast's economy and society for the next 50 years. Coal was extracted from mines in remote and mountainous areas by a variety of rope, tram and rail transport systems. By the 1950s West Coast coal mining was declining as the most accessible coal was mined out. By the 1990s new technology had increased coal production again. Today's mines are much larger and more efficient, but provide fewer jobs.

Forestry: Logging and milling of the West Coast's native forests began in the 1860s as a result of the gold rushes. The Coast's first timber mill was built at Hokitika in 1865, where timber was in great demand for buildings. The towns of Hokitika and Greymouth sprang up almost overnight. The underground quartz gold mines (after 1870s) and coal mines (after 1890s) increased the local demand for timber. Timber milling reached a peak in the 1960s. Since then environmental concerns have restricted logging of native forests. Plantation forests of exotic pines have been planted to try and retain a timber industry on the West Coast.

A future for conservation?
Westland National Park was created in 1960, extending from the highest peaks of the Southern Alps down to the Tasman Sea. The Park includes glaciers, lakes, rivers, forests and old gold-mining sites. Tourist activity is centred on the glacier settlements of Franz Josef and Fox.

Paparoa National Park is one of the smallest national parks in New Zealand. It was created in 1987 to preserve its unique limestone landscapes, including the famous 'Pancake Rocks' at Punakaiki. Inland the 'karst' landscape is riddled with narrow gorges, collapsed caverns, caves and underground streams.

World Heritage Area: Southwest New Zealand, Te Wahi Pounamu, was given World Heritage status by the United Nations in 1990. It was recognised as one of the world's great forest and mountain wildernesses areas, and protects South Westland's lowland forests from logging.

Eco-tourism offers tourists more than just scenic views. It offers experiences that help tourists understand local ecology without harming it. Tourists are offered guided walks, cruises and tours to see a wide variety of birds (penguins, kotuku), mammals (dolphins, seals), insects (glow-worms), trees (beech, rimu, kahikatea) and landforms (glaciers, limestone features). Guided eco-tour groups are generally small and make little impact on the environment.

Heritage tourism: The West Coast's mining and logging heritage is now part of its tourist attraction. Tourists can pan for gold, explore reconstructed shanty towns and visit old mine sites.

Adventure tourism: Tourists seeking adventure can choose from white-water rafting, black-water rafting, kayaking, jet boating, caving, mountaineering, glacier walking and sky diving!

Recreational tourism: Hunting and fishing are popular activities for locals and tourists.

SOUTH ISLAND

DID YOU KNOW?

- **Underground explosions** are a major hazard in coal mines. Sixty-five miners were killed in the Brunner Mine disaster of 1896; nineteen were killed in an explosion in the Strongman Mine in 1967.
- **Sphagnum moss** from West Coast swamps is exported all the way to Japan!
- **Reefton** is recognised as the first town in the southern hemisphere to have electric lighting. The first permanent lights were turned on in 1888 when Reefton was a booming gold town.
- **The small West Coast town** of Blackball (450 residents) is known as the birthplace of the New Zealand Labour Party. In 1908 its striking coal miners won a battle for a longer lunch break and an eight-hour working day. Their success encouraged the trade union movement and eventually led to the formation of the Labour Party.
- **Hokitika's** annual Wild Foods Festival provides a feast of Kiwi bush tucker, including huhu grubs and worms!
- **New Zealand's** largest gold nugget was found at Ross in 1909. 'The Honourable Roddy', as it was called, weighed 3.1 kg.
- **Colliers Creek**, in Westland, holds the New Zealand record of 682 mm for the highest rainfall recorded in one day. It was a summer's day in January 1994!
- **The highest rainfall** recorded in New Zealand in one year was 16,617 mm at Cropp River, also in Westland, in 1998.

SOUTH ISLAND

West Coast – Natural Forces at Work

The Alpine Fault and Westland National Park's glaciers represent two powerful and competing forces of nature – uplift and erosion.

The Alpine Fault is the birthplace of the South Island, a collision zone in the earth's fragile crust. The struggle between the Pacific Plate (to the east) and the Australian Plate (to the west) has thrust up the high mountains of the South Island. The glaciers that have formed on the mountains are wearing them down again. Nature's powerful forces are at work.

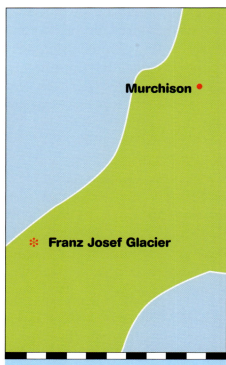

QUICK FACTS:
- The Alpine Fault runs for 600 km from Fiordland to Marlborough.
- Major earthquakes occurred at Murchison in 1929 and Inangahua in 1968.
- There are 140 glaciers in Westland National Park.
- The Franz Josef and Fox glaciers are the Park's largest glaciers.
- No other glaciers at the same latitude reach such a low altitude.

The Alpine Fault is clearly visible from the air, slicing into the South Island at Milford Sound and splintering into several smaller faults before disappearing into Cook Strait. Moving at a few centimetres a year, the Pacific Plate moves towards the west while the Australian Plate slips by towards the northeast.

Earthquakes
The collision of the two plates builds up great stress in the rocks along the Alpine Fault. When the stress gets too much the rocks break or shift, and we have an earthquake. Small earthquakes happen nearly all the time. Thankfully large ones are less frequent.

Murchison: The 1929 earthquake at Murchison measured 7.8 on the Richter scale and caused widespread damage. Seventeen people were killed, mainly by landslips triggered by the earthquake.

Inangahua: The Inangahua earthquake of 1968 measured 7.1 on the Richter scale and was felt over most of the South Island. Two people were killed by one landslip and the Buller River was temporarily blocked by another.

Glaciers
A glacier is sometimes described as a very slow-moving 'river of ice'. When large quantities of permanent snow accumulate in a high mountain basin, the lower layers of snow are compacted into solid ice. When the

weight of snow and ice moves the ice slowly downhill a glacier is born. As long as the supply of snow continues at its source, the glacier will continue to 'flow' downhill.

Franz Josef Glacier ice moves forward at between 1.5 and 4 m a day. The Waiho River flows from the melting 'snout' of the Franz Josef Glacier. Huge quantities of moraine are released.

Huge amounts of snow accumulate on the high mountains of Westland National Park. This névé feeds the 140 glaciers that carve their way down through the Park's valleys. With rocks frozen into their bases the glaciers act like coarse sandpaper and erode valley floors and sides. The eroded material carried by a glacier is called moraine.

When a glacier snout retreats, moraine is spread evenly over the valley floor. When a snout remains stationary for a period of time its deposits build up to form a terminal moraine. Franz Josef's Waiho Loop, formed 12,000 years ago, is a fine example of a terminal moraine. Imagine how large the glacier was then!

Advance or retreat?

In the last ice age Westland's glaciers reached the sea and released icebergs! Since then the climate has warmed and the glaciers have retreated. But it has not been a steady retreat and there have been three advances since 1940. Tourists today have much further to walk to reach the ice than they did 50 years ago. Heavier than usual snowfall at the top of the Franz Josef and Fox glaciers causes their snouts to advance about five or six years later. Lower than usual snowfall has the opposite effect and the glaciers' snouts retreat. The last advance began in 1982 and has moved the Franz Josef snout forward more than one kilometre!

SOUTH ISLAND

DID YOU KNOW?

- **Millions of years ago** the rocks of northwest Nelson were part of Fiordland. Over millions of years they have been carried northeast by the movement of the Australian Plate. If this movement continues Nelson may eventually become part of the North Island!
- **The Inangahua earthquake** was the sixteenth earthquake over 7 on the Richter scale in New Zealand since 1848.
- **In 1865** Julius von Haast, an Austrian geologist and explorer, named the Franz Josef Glacier after the Austrian emperor of the time.
- **Ice and snow** at the top of the Franz Josef and Fox glaciers is estimated to be up to 300 m thick.
- **What the glaciers** take away at the top they give back at the bottom. The bed of the Waiho River is being built up so quickly with moraine from the glacier that the road bridge across it will eventually have to be raised!

Postcard from the West Coast

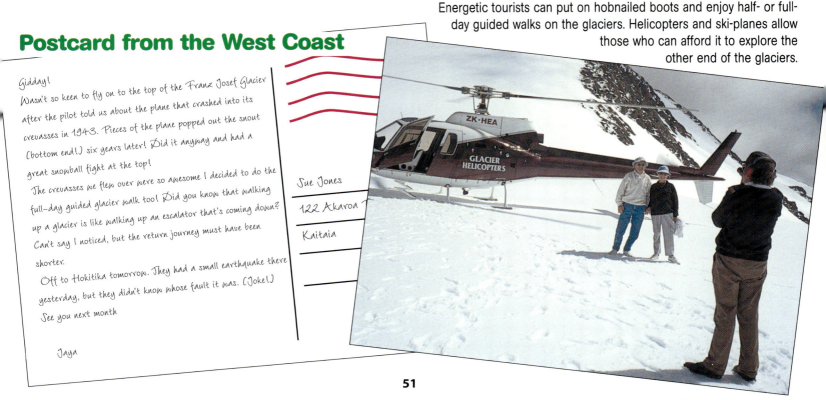

Energetic tourists can put on hobnailed boots and enjoy half- or full-day guided walks on the glaciers. Helicopters and ski-planes allow those who can afford it to explore the other end of the glaciers.

Gidday!
Wasn't so keen to fly on to the top of the Franz Josef Glacier after the pilot told us about the plane that crashed into its crevasses in 1943. Pieces of the plane popped out the snout (bottom end!) six years later! Did it anyway and had a great snowball fight at the top!
The crevasses we flew over were so awesome I decided to do the full-day guided glacier walk too! Did you know that walking up a glacier is like walking up an escalator that's coming down? Can't say I noticed, but the return journey must have been shorter.
Off to Hokitika tomorrow. They had a small earthquake there yesterday, but they didn't know whose fault it was. (Joke!)
See you next month

Jaya

Sue Jones
122 Akaroa
Kaitaia

51

SOUTH ISLAND

Fiordland – World Heritage Area

Mitre Peak rises almost vertically from Milford Sound for 1692 m, more than any other coastal mountain in the world. It is typical of Fiordland's magnificent ice-sculpted, rain-drenched landscape. Milford Sound is now the most visited of New Zealand's coastal fiords, but it was missed by Captain Cook when he sailed past in 1770. Its entrance is screened from view by its headlands.

The need to preserve Fiordland's natural landscape was recognised by New Zealanders when Fiordland National Park was created in 1952. In 1990 it received world recognition with its inclusion in the Southwest New Zealand/Te Wahi Pounamu World Heritage Area.

Dramatic landscapes

Fiordland's mountains have been scraped and scoured by hundreds of glaciers to produce today's spectacular U-shaped valleys, plunging waterfalls, deep blue fiords and high mountain lakes. Drenched by metres of rainfall each year, all but the steepest slopes are covered by dense forest or alpine tussock grass.

Doubtful Sound: (below left) In 1770 Captain Cook had doubts about sailing into one of Fiordland's 'sounds' in case there was no wind to sail out on. He named it Doubtful Sound. Fiordland's sounds are actually fiords. Like the fiords of Norway, they were carved out by glaciers when the sea level was lower, and have since filled with water.

Sutherland Falls: (centre) Once thought the highest falls in the world, the water from Lake Quill falls 580 m in three spectacular leaps. The falls are named after Donald Sutherland, the first European to see them.

QUICK FACTS:

- Fiordland is New Zealand's largest national park (approx 1.3 million ha).
- Fiordland is mainland New Zealand's most remote area.

EVENTS CALENDAR:

April:
Milford Track closes
October:
Milford Track opens

Lake Te Anau: (below right) The lake is named after the glow-worm caves on its far shore. The lake's western 'fingers' reach a depth of 417 m, over 200 m below sea level! At the northern end of the lake, accessible only by boat, is the start of the Milford Track.

Walking wonderland

Milford Track: (above) This track takes walkers through steep-sided valleys, past cascading waterfalls and over the spectacular Mackinnon Pass to Milford Sound – and its sandflies! The only way to avoid them is to keep on walking!
Routeburn Track: This track is more accessible than the Milford Track and therefore much busier. Much of the track is through alpine tussocks, high above the treeline, giving spectacular views of Fiordland's snow-capped mountains and forested valleys.

Human impact

Fiordland's climate and remoteness have defeated most attempts to tame its rugged beauty. Future development is likely to be very strictly controlled in order to preserve its unique wilderness character.
Homer Tunnel: The Homer Tunnel opened up Milford Sound to tourism. It was proposed in 1899, begun in 1935 and finished in 1952. Nothing is easy in Fiordland! Special 'portals' have been built over the tunnel entrances to shelter them from frequent avalanches.
Manapouri Power Station: In the 1960s there was a plan to build a hydro-electric power station on Lake Manapouri, which would raise the level of the lake. It started one of New Zealand's biggest ever environmental protests. After a change of government the plan was changed. A largely hidden underground power station was built, allowing the lake to more or less keep its natural level.

Flightless birds

Takahe: The takahe was thought to be extinct until its rediscovery in Fiordland's Murchison Mountains in 1948. A takahe reserve has been established and with the help of a breeding programme there are now about 180 takahe.
Kakapo: The flightless, heavyweight kakapo is the world's largest parrot. Its future now depends on the success of breeding programmes established on rat-free offshore islands.
Kiwi: Fiordland's two varieties of kiwi are more likely to be heard than seen as they are flightless and nocturnal. Introduced animals like cats, rats, stoats and dogs, and forest clearance, have reduced the kiwi population by 95 per cent over the past 1000 years.
Fiordland crested penguin: Fiordland's very own penguin is a very snappy dresser. Its white shirt and blue-black jacket are topped by brilliant orange lipstick and a striking blondstreaked hairdo! Small and shy, its call has been described as the sound of a nail scratching rusty roofing iron.

Takahe.

Kiwi.

Fiordland crested penguin.

SOUTH ISLAND

DID YOU KNOW?

- **Fiordland** is the most remote and least touched part of New Zealand's mainland. Only one public road reaches its vast coastline.
- **The road** to the Homer Tunnel is claimed to be the world's most avalanche-prone road, thanks to heavy winter snowfalls and almost vertical valley walls.
- **Manapouri's** underground power station, 213 m below the surface, is reached by a two kilometre spiral tunnel. The gradient of the road is a very steep 1:10.
- **Thanks to Fiordland's** very heavy rainfall, a layer of fresh water covers most of Milford Sound. Stained by tannin from the forests, this darker water filters out sunlight and allows deep-water creatures to survive close to the surface.
- **The small town of Te Anau** has been called the 'walking capital of the world'. It is the nearest town to many walking tracks, including the world-famous Milford Track.
- **Fiordland's** fresh water is considered to be so pure that it is bottled and sold around the world as a healthy mineral water.

SOUTH ISLAND

The Far South – Oysters and Aluminium

Bluff is New Zealand's other 'Land's End' and a long way from most places! It originally served as a trading post for whalers and sealers. Today it is the main port of Southland. Port activities, its fishing fleet, fish processing factories and the nearby Tiwai Point aluminium smelter sustain its people.

The Far South was the centre of early European settler activity, but it has long since been left behind as people, politics and business moved north. From 1986 to 1996 Southland's population declined by over 10 per cent. This 'forgotten corner' of New Zealand, however, contains some of its 'best kept secrets'.

QUICK FACTS:
- Invercargill (population 49,000) is the Far South's main urban centre.
- Southland's population declined by over 10 per cent between 1986 and 1996.
- The Far South's economy is based on farming, fishing, forestry, mining and aluminium smelting.
- In summer the sun sets later in Southland than in any other part of New Zealand.

EVENTS CALENDAR:
January:
Wild Challenge
(97 km run/canoe/bike) at Tuatapere
February:
Hokonui Moonshine Whisky Festival
May:
New Zealand Gold Guitar Awards, Gore

People

Despite their isolation, or maybe because of it, the people of the Far South are proud of their heritage. They have a reputation for friendliness and hospitality, a distinctive accent with its 'Southland burr' and a liking for country music.

Invercargill, the 'Friendly City', has fine parks and well laid out streets, but it is steadily losing people to the big cities further north.

Southland's Scottish heritage brought with it both a love of whisky and a strict law-abiding character. These two came into conflict when liquor prohibition in the 1920s made whisky distilling illegal. Distillers went into hiding in the Hokonui Hills and 'moonshining' maintained the flow of whisky!

Gore comes alive to the sound of country music at the New Zealand Gold Guitar Awards festival. The festival attracts country musicians from all around New Zealand and overseas.

Farming
Southland has always been associated with farming. Meat and wool have always been

important, and in the 1880s Southland became the first region to export dairy products. A little over 100 years later dairying is regaining its importance in Southland.

The hills and river flats of northern Southland produce fine wools, and the plains further south fatten lambs and cattle for meat.

Edendale was the site of New Zealand's first dairy factory. In 1882 its owners won a prize of £500 from the government for being the first to successfully export 50 tons of cheese. Butter exports followed soon after. Its farmers were some of the first to use artificial fertilisers to boost production.

Mossburn has been called New Zealand's deer capital. It was one of the first areas to take up deer farming.

Fishing

Southland is known around the world for its fishing. Bluff means only one thing to gourmets – oysters! The Mataura River is equally well known among anglers for its brown trout.

Gore, on the banks of the Mataura River, is considered by many to be New Zealand's brown trout capital.

Bluff is the home of the famous Bluff oyster. The oysters are harvested from the floor of Foveaux Strait. They are shelled and packed locally before being rushed, fresh, to restaurants and supermarkets around New Zealand and overseas.

Minerals

Although the far south is best known for its agriculture, minerals have played an important part in its development. Gold mining came first, followed by coal mining and now aluminium smelting. Southland's huge deposits of coal were first mined in the 1880s and by 1903 were producing 30 per cent of New Zealand's coal output. With higher grade coal available elsewhere in New Zealand, Southland now produces little more than 10 per cent of the national output. Falling demand and mechanised open-cast mining techniques have slashed employment levels, and coal mining communities have suffered.

Abundant cheap hydroelectric power from the Manapouri Power Station (see page 53) was the key to an aluminium smelter being established at remote Tiwai Point. Alumina (refined bauxite) comes in from Queensland and aluminium goes out to industries around New Zealand and overseas.

The Catlins

A popular travel guide advises visitors to the hills, forests and coastline of 'the Catlins' to allow twice as much time as they think they'll need.

The magnificent Cathedral Caves are

SOUTH ISLAND

DID YOU KNOW?

- **Southland Museum** in Invercargill has New Zealand's only 'tuatarium'. It holds the biggest collection of tuatara in the world. Some of the tuatara, the only surviving species from the age of the dinosaurs, are over 100 years old.
- **Continuously settled** since 1824, Bluff claims to be the oldest European settlement in the country.
- **About 70 per cent** of New Zealand's coal reserves are in Southland.
- **180 million-year-old** petrified (fossilised) trees are exposed at low tide at Curio Bay on 'the Catlins' coast. You can still count the age rings in the fossilised tree stumps!
- **The eight-storey viaduct** at Percy Burn is said to be the oldest wooden railway bridge in the world.
- **Maori oral history** records that the ancestral Takitimu canoe from Hawaiki ran aground at the mouth of the Waiau River, near Tuatapere.

only accessible at low tide. There are many other hidden secrets along the Catlins' rocky, bush-fringed coast, where fur seals, yellow-eyed penguins, Hooker sealions and Hector's dolphins can be seen.

SOUTH ISLAND

Dunedin – Edinburgh of the South

The Octagon is Dunedin's unusual, eight-sided city centre. Its geometrical design seems appropriate for a university town.

Dunedin began as 'New Edinburgh' in 1847 with the arrival of 344 Scottish settlers. Most were members of the Presbyterian Church. The new settlement developed slowly until the Central Otago gold rushes of the 1860s. Dunedin's banks and businesses boomed and it soon became the commercial capital of New Zealand. It is now a much quieter regional centre.

Dunedin's Victorian architecture reflects its 'golden' days towards the end of the nineteenth century. Larnach Castle (above) was built for the chief manager of the Bank of Otago in 1871. The grand Municipal Chambers were built in 1880.

Preachers and pubs

Gold miners were generally heavy drinkers and Dunedin's Presbyterian Christians struggled for years to prohibit or restrict the manufacture, sale or drinking of alcohol. Between 1886 and 1927 about half of Dunedin's hotels lost their liquor licences.

The Octagon's statue of Scottish poet Robbie Burns (built in 1887) celebrates the city's Scottish heritage. The poet's Presbyterian nephew, the Reverend Thomas Burns, was among the first settlers to arrive from Scotland. Wilson's Whisky Distillery, the only one in New Zealand, reflects a quite different aspect of Dunedin's Scottish heritage.

QUICK FACTS:

- Dunedin (population 112,000) is New Zealand's fifth largest city.
- The city is built on an ancient and extinct volcanic centre.
- Dunedin's climate is cool and wet.
- Dunedin's main port is Port Chalmers, 12 km up-harbour.
- Its economy is based on service industries, food processing and the manufacture of woollen goods, footwear and agricultural machinery.

EVENTS CALENDAR:

January:
Albatross eggs hatch at Taiaroa Head
February:
Dunedin Festival
March:
Scottish Week celebrates Dunedin's Highland heritage
October:
Rhododendron Festival
November:
World Stone Sawing Championships, Oamaru

Otago Peninsula

The Otago Peninsula has earned Dunedin the reputation as New Zealand's 'wildlife capital'. It is home to colonies of seals, penguins and albatrosses.

Education

Dunedin is well known for its educational institutions, some of which were established in the nineteenth century. Today its university trains many of the country's doctors and dentists.

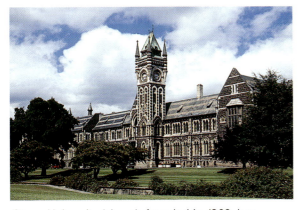

Otago University (above), founded in 1869, has retained many of its original stone buildings. The impressive bluestone buildings of Otago Boys High School were built in 1884.

Dunedin's 'scarfies' (university students) give the city a lively atmosphere, particularly at capping (graduation week) and rugby matches!

Albatross colony: Taiaroa Head, at the end of the Otago Peninsula, is the world's only mainland albatross colony. Ten other species of bird breed on this protected, but windswept, headland. Viewing of the royal albatrosses is restricted during the breeding season from September to November each year.

Yellow-eyed penguins: Fires, predators and land development had reduced the population of the world's rarest penguin to an estimated 160 breeding pairs in 1990. The yellow-eyed penguin, or hoiho, can be viewed from specially designed 'hides' at several penguin reserves along the southern coast of the Otago Peninsula. Their nests can be as far as one kilometre from the shore.

Seals: Colonies of New Zealand fur seals are often best viewed from the sea. Seals were once slaughtered along this coast for their skins, but they are now protected.

Aquarium: Life under the sea can be explored at the Marine Aquarium, Portobello. Touch tanks allow visitors to make contact with marine animals. The University of Otago maintains a laboratory here for marine research.

Beyond Dunedin

Taieri Gorge Railway: Dunedin had one of the world's earliest cable tramway systems, but it was gone by 1957. The Taieri Gorge Railway, which dates back to 1879, takes travellers out to Pukerangi and much further back in time.

Moeraki boulders: The remarkable boulders that litter the beach at Moeraki are now protected

as a scientific reserve. Although they have been eroded out of the cliffs behind the beach, they were originally formed under the sea. The largest boulders have a circumference of over 4 m.

Gold mining: Gold is once again being mined in Otago, but the methods are quite different from those used in the 1860s. The Round Hill open-cast mine at Macraes Flat uses massive earth-moving machinery to extract gold-bearing rock. It is now New Zealand's most productive gold mine.

Oamaru: A little more than 100 km north of Dunedin lies Oamaru. Once a busy port, it is now better known for its 'urban' penguins, its distinctive cream-coloured stone architecture and the World Stone Sawing Championships it hosts each year!

SOUTH ISLAND

DID YOU KNOW?

- **The name 'Otago'** is derived from the Maori settlement of Otakou, situated near the end of the Otago Peninsula.
- **Dunedin** is the original Gaelic name for Edinburgh. It replaced the name New Edinburgh.
- **Thomas Bracken**, who wrote the national anthem *God Defend New Zealand* in 1890, was from Dunedin.
- **Dunedin's Baldwin** Street is claimed as the world's steepest street. It has a gradient of about 1:1! Certainly no place to learn the art of roller-blading!
- **Dunedin** has New Zealand's only kilt shop. Och aye!
- **Royal albatrosses** at Taiaroa Head can circumnavigate the world without once touching down on land!
- **The world's first** frozen meat exports were processed at Totara Estate between Dunedin and Oamaru in 1882.

SOUTH ISLAND

Central Otago – Golden Heritage

Arrowtown.

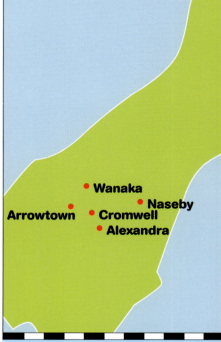

Central Otago's dry tussock grasslands attracted settlers seeking land for grazing sheep. People followed in their thousands when gold was found in its mighty rivers in the 1860s. Those rivers were later dammed for electricity and orchards flourished in the hot sunny summers and cold dry winters. Today, holidaymakers flock to its rivers, lakes and mountains in both summer and winter.

QUICK FACTS:
- Cromwell, Wanaka and Alexandra are the main towns.
- Central Otago is New Zealand's driest region.
- Cromwell is further from the sea than any other South Island town.
- Ophir holds the record for the lowest recorded temperature, -21.6° C.

EVENTS CALENDAR:
January:
Wanaka Rodeo
February:
Central Otago A & P Show
April:
Warbirds Over Wanaka air show (every second Easter)
June:
Brass Monkey motorbike rally, Oturehua
September:
Blossom Festival, Alexandra
Wanaka Snowfest

Gold

The Otago 'gold rush' was short-lived. Once the most accessible gold had been taken the rush was reversed, but Central Otago was on the map. By the 1890s hundreds of large dredges were extracting gold from Otago's river beds. In the 1990s new mining technology was drawing gold-mining companies back to Central Otago. There's still plenty of gold there! The Shotover River was described as the 'richest river in the world' and gold-diggers arrived in a hurry from all around the world. Fortunes were made and lost in only a few years. Often it was the hotel owners who made more money than the miners themselves.

By the 1880s only patient Chinese miners, some reworking old diggings, and Europeans with the capital to buy new mining technology, remained. The Clyde Dam project flooded many old Chinese miners' settlements. Reconstructed Chinese shelters along the banks of the Kawarau River reflect the hardships they had to endure.

Power

Central Otago may be New Zealand's driest region but it is not short of water. Heavy rains and melting snows from the Southern Alps supply its mighty rivers and large lakes.

Lake Hawea is the third largest of Central Otago's natural lakes, after Wakatipu and Wanaka. These lakes contribute to (and control) the flow of water into the South Island's largest river, the Clutha. When the Roxburgh Dam and hydroelectric power station was completed in 1962 it was the largest in the country.

Lake Dunstan was created by the Clyde Dam near Cromwell. The Clutha River backs up behind the dam for 26 km, raising the water level by about 60 m. The dam was planned in 1977, but not completed until 1994. It remains controversial. There are concerns about active faults causing earthquakes and landslips. A large area of productive orchard land and part of old Cromwell were lost when Lake Dunstan was filled.

Water sprays can help prevent serious fruit damage by late spring frosts. Cold winters provide the chilling needed for bud burst, and endless summer sunshine ripens the fruit.

Cromwell's 'statue of four fruits' celebrates Central Otago's orchard heritage. Orchards were first established here by miners during the 1860s gold rush. More recently New Zealand's southernmost vineyards have been established near Cromwell and Alexandra.

Holiday fun

Central Otago is the South Island's premier tourist destination. Visitors from New Zealand and overseas are attracted in their thousands by its spectacular landscape, reliable climate and its cultural heritage.

Holiday centre:

Like Queenstown (see pages 60-61), Wanaka attracts visitors all year round. In summer, watersports and fishing are popular on Wanaka's lakes and rivers, and campers and trampers head to the mountains of Mount Aspiring National Park. In winter, skiers and snowboarders flock to skifields at Treble Cone and Cardrona.

Airshow: The biennial international airshow, Warbirds Over Wanaka, has been described as one of the best air shows in the world. The show takes place at Wanaka Airport where the New Zealand Fighter Pilot Museum and the Wanaka Transport Museum are located. The air show and the museums take advantage of Wanaka's dry climate and clear skies.

Puzzling world: People of all ages are puzzled by Wanaka's 3-D maze and tilted house. Getting lost in the maze and watching a billiard ball roll 'uphill' unaided are just two of Puzzling World's many highlights.

SOUTH ISLAND

DID YOU KNOW?

- **Over 400 dredges** have operated in Central Otago's rivers since the 1890s.
- **Cromwell's** town centre was rebuilt on higher ground when the Clyde Dam and Lake Dunstan flooded the old town in 1992.
- **Central Otago** experiences New Zealand's greatest seasonal variation in temperature – freezing winters and burning summers!
- **The Maniototo Ice Rink** in Naseby is the largest artificial outdoor ice rink in New Zealand. Ice usually lasts from May to September.

Fruit

Well away from the sea, Central Otago enjoys a 'continental' climate. It is renowned for its orchards of stone fruits. Cherries, apricots, plums and peaches thrive in its hot sunny summers and cold dry winters.

Central Otago's rivers and lakes provide ample water for irrigation in summer.

Heritage tourism: Many of Central Otago's small towns have held on to some of their gold rush heritage, and they add to the region's tourist appeal.

SOUTH ISLAND

Queenstown – Adventure Capital

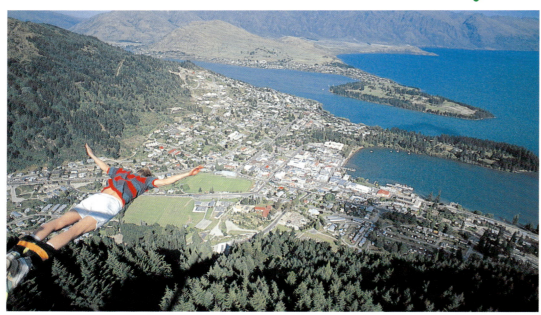

Queenstown is the home of bungy jumping. People from far and wide willingly pay good money to fall 100 m off a ledge, bridge, platform (anywhere high and scary enough!) with an elastic cord tied round their ankles. Survivors proudly wear their souvenir T-shirts and take videotaped proof of their bravado away with them.

Queenstown is New Zealand's premier tourist centre, attracting a wide range of tourists all year round. It has something for everyone, from the sedate tour-bus type to the adrenalin-pumping thrillseeker.

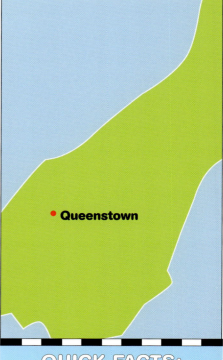

QUICK FACTS:
- The Queenstown-Lakes area is one of New Zealand's fastest growing districts.
- Lake Wakatipu is New Zealand's third largest lake.
- Much of Lake Wakatipu is over 350 m deep.
- Queenstown has a dry 'continental' climate – hot in summer and cold in winter

EVENTS CALENDAR:
January:
Wine and Food Festival
June:
Winter Festival

History

The first Europeans who stumbled across Lake Wakatipu in the 1850s saw it as good sheep grazing country. The gold rush of the 1860s put Queenstown on the map but it was settlers with sheep who led the way.

From the 1880s steamships on Lake Wakatipu kept the large sheep 'stations' supplied and took out their wool. By the early 1900s the railway line from Invercargill, connecting with steamships at Kingston, was bringing holidaymakers to Queenstown. The

SS *Earnslaw* (pictured), which was built in 1912, is the last remaining steamship on Lake Wakatipu. The 'Kingston Flyer' train, like the Earnslaw, now runs only for tourists.

Summer thrills and spills

Queenstown was founded by the gold rush, but it is an adrenalin rush that attracts many of its visitors today. With good reason Queenstown is known as the 'world's adventure capital'.

SOUTH ISLAND

White-water rafting: If you didn't get wet bungy jumping you will when you go white-water rafting on Queenstown's thrilling Shotover or Kawarau rivers. Furious paddling to the guide's shouted instructions helps take your mind off the looming rapids!

Skydiving: For those who want to stay dry while they are being thrilled, bungy cords can be exchanged for parachutes. Tandem skydiving from a plane at 2000-3 000 m or paragliding off a mountainside are two ways of keeping dry!

Winter wonderland

Queenstown's Winter Festival signals the start of the snow season. With two local ski-fields to choose from, Queenstown has become New Zealand's winter sports capital.

Coronet Peak: Coronet Peak is Queenstown's most popular skifield. Night skiing has recently added to its attraction.

Remarkables: The most recent of Queenstown's three skifields, tucked in behind the Remarkables Range.

Cardrona: Cardrona is particularly popular with family groups. Across the valley lies New Zealand's premier cross-country skiing terrain.

Jet boating: Jet boating through Queenstown's river canyons is not for the faint-hearted! It's not exactly quiet eco-tourism, but you certainly have a better appreciation of life when you get back on dry land!

DID YOU KNOW?

- **According to** one Maori legend, the crooked shape of Lake Wakatipu represents the folded body of a giant, burnt for stealing another's lover.
- **Queenstown's** thoughtful jet boat operators pump hot water through the safety rails of their boats to ensure that joyriders can hold on tight, even in mid-winter!
- **When jet boats** get up speed they need only a few centimetres of water to operate in. This allows them to 'miraculously' glide over the shallowest of rapids.
- **Lake Wakatipu** must have royalty in its blood! At one end of the lake is Kingston; Queenstown lies across the water; and looking down from above are Coronet Peak and the Crown Range.
- **Heavy rain** in the mountains around Queenstown can raise the level of Lake Wakatipu. In 1878 and 1999 floodwaters invaded waterfront shops and boats sailed through the streets.

If you prefer to keep your feet 'on the ground' when you go up in the air, then Queenstown's Skyline Gondola is for you. If views of the jagged Remarkables Range across the lake don't take your breath away, then the luge ride back down to Queenstown will!

Postcard from Queenstown

Hi, guys
I've got to get outta here — it's exhausting! I've done all those crazy things I said I'd never do, like bungy jumping, white-water rafting and sky-diving! Today I decided to do something pretty relaxed for a change and took a ride up the gondola. Awesome views — you can see how the Remarkables Range got its name. Anyway, when I got to the top I saw these crazy guys shooting down the mountain on what they call luges. That was the end of relaxation for me! I just had to have a go — or six! First-timers go down a learners' track and then you can really let rip on the advanced track.
That's Queenstown for you — one rush after another!

Ricky

Mr Smith
7a Turnbu
Devonpo

61

SOUTH ISLAND

Mackenzie Country – Tussock, Turbines and Tourists

Mackenzie country is named after James McKenzie. In 1885 he was caught red-handed with 1000 sheep he didn't own and was jailed. After repeated escapes he was finally pardoned on the con-dition he left the country. His legend is now larger than his life ever was. The dry, tussocky grasslands he was heading for when he was captured now bear his name (albeit spelt differently).

Access to the Mackenzie country is either along the valley of the Waitaki River or over one of its several mountain passes. Sheltered by mountains the region experiences little rainfall. Its tussock grasslands were once thought to be good for only sheep, but since the 1960s it has produced vast amounts of hydroelectricity and attracts increasing numbers of tourists.

Sheep farming

The Mackenzie country will always be associated with sheep farming. The earliest 'runholders' came with their flocks in the 1850s and for about one hundred years they dominated the economy of the Mackenzie.

(below left) The merino, which thrives in the dry tussocks of the Mackenzie country, produces the finest wool in the world.
(centre) The bronze statue by the shores of Lake Tekapo is a reminder that without the help of the sheep dog 'the grazing of the mountain-ous country would be impossible'.
(below right) The Church of the Good Shepherd, built in 1935 was a tribute to the hardy pioneers who introduced sheep to the Mackenzie country.

QUICK FACTS:
- Four mountain passes and one river valley lead into the Mackenzie country.
- Twizel is the main town, while Fairlie is the 'gateway' to the Mackenzie country.
- The economy is based on sheep farming, power generation and tourism.
- The climate is hot and dry in summer and cold and dry in winter.

EVENTS CALENDAR:
April:
Mackenzie Highland Show (Easter Monday), Fairlie
Maadi Cup – NZ schools rowing championships, Twizel
July:
Ski season begins in surrounding mountains
December:
Mackenzie Shears, shearing contest, Fairlie

SOUTH ISLAND

DID YOU KNOW?

- **Four mountain passes** give access to the Mackenzie country. From north to south they are Burke, Mackenzie, Hakataramea and Lindis.
- **The Waitaki Dam** was completed in 1936. It was the last hydro-dam in New Zealand to be built by old-fashioned pick and shovel methods.
- **Mount John's** American satellite tracking station has sometimes been the target of peace activists suspicious about its military potential.
- **Salmon farms** have been established in the cold, clean water of the Upper Waitaki Power Scheme's canals.
- **Lake Pukaki's** turqoise-blue colour is typical of glacier-fed lakes. The water carries fine 'rock-flour', produced by the grinding action of glacier ice. Stream-fed lakes are clearer and warmer.

Waitaki power schemes

It may not rain very much in the Mackenzie country, but it is not short of water. Heavy snow and rainfall in the Southern Alps drains away through lakes Ohau, Pukaki and Tekapo into the Waitaki River. The Waitaki power schemes harness this flow of water to generate hydroelectricity from eight power stations.

Upper Waitaki: Spring snow-melt is stored in lakes Tekapo, Pukaki and Ohau for electricity generation in winter. A network of canals carries the water to a series of power stations – Tekapo A and B, and Ohau A, B and C on the Upper Waitaki River.

Lower Waitaki: Lake Benmore is the largest of three lakes created by dams on the Lower Waitaki River. The other two are Lake Aviemore and Lake Waitaki. The Waitaki Dam was the first of eight hydro-electric power stations to be built on the Waitaki River and its tributaries. The lakes are popular for watersports and fishing.

Irrigation: The Waitaki's hydro schemes have created an irrigated farming boom. The canals and their steady supply of water have transformed areas previously too dry for intensive farming.

Twizel

The town of Twizel was built in the 1960s to house workers from the Upper Waitaki hydro scheme. When the dams and power stations were completed in the 1980s the town, like the black stilt, was threatened with extinction. The town refused to die and it has been reinvented as a tourist centre, taking advantage of its sunny climate and nearby skifields, lakes and rivers.

Black stilt: Development of the Mackenzie country has brought the small black stilt (left) to the brink of extinction. Introduced predators (including cats, ferrets and rats) and disturbance of its river-flat habitat (by hydro schemes and farming) had reduced its numbers to about 50 adults by the 1980s. A recovery programme is now run by the Department of Conservation near Twizel.

Clear skies

Clear skies attract both astronomers and gliders from around the world to the Mackenzie country. Omarama, in the lee of the Southern Alps and warmed by consistent summer sunshine, has ideal conditions for gliding. Enthusiasts come from around the world to silently soar in its rising thermals. Spectacular views of turquoise lakes and snow-capped Mount Cook is just the 'icing on the cake'.

The international observatory built at Mount John in 1965 is run by the University of Canterbury and two American universities. Cloudless skies, incredibly clear atmosphere and powerful telescopes make it an ideal base for astronomical research.

SOUTH ISLAND

Canterbury – Patchwork Plains

A deep layer of rock and gravel deposits carpet the Canterbury Plains. They were eroded from the Southern Alps by ice age glaciers and deposited at the foot of the mountains by melting ice, rivers and wind. The glaciers have since retreated and braided rivers now twist their way through the gently sloping plains to the sea.

The Canterbury Plains were once forested and home to large numbers of moa. By the time European settlers arrived in the nineteenth century, the plains were covered mainly in tussock grasses. European runholders grazed sheep on the plains until wheat farms transformed the landscape in the 1870s. By the early 1900s the plains had been transformed again. Railways, irrigation systems, the use of artificial fertilisers and the export of frozen meat produced a landscape of smaller 'mixed farms', which fattened lambs and grew a variety of crops.

QUICK FACTS:
- Christchurch (population 331,000) is the main urban centre.
- Timaru (28,000) is an important port town in the south.
- The Canterbury Plains are the largest plains in New Zealand.
- The economy of the plains is based on mixed sheep and crop farming.
- The climate of the plains is generally dry, with hot summers and cold winters.

Maori rock drawings have been found at several places around the edge of the Canterbury Plains. They frequently show moa, a now extinct, flightless bird. Moa, especially giant moa, were an important part of the diet for early Maori. Being flightless, they were fairly easy prey – trapped in gullies, chased over cliffs or flushed out of bush by fire. Hunting moa by fire is thought to be one reason why the Canterbury Plains lost their forests. Hot, dry and violent, Canterbury's nor'wester winds can wreak havoc as they blow down from the Southern Alps. When nor'westers blow, 'arch' clouds often form over the mountains, and people's moods can be adversely affected.

The high mountains of the Southern Alps cast a long 'rain shadow' over the Canterbury Plains. As a result most of the plains receive less than 800 mm of rain each year. Farmers on the plains now depend on irrigation water taken from rivers and carried to farms along water 'races'. The first races were built near Ashburton in the 1860s, not far from the present day irrigation research centre.

Roads, railways and property boundaries were ruled in straight lines across New Zealand's largest plain. Long, dark belts of pine trees, planted to provide shelter from Canterbury's nor'wester winds, emphasised the patchwork appearance of the plains.

Lincoln University specialises in agri-

cultural research and training. Founded as Canterbury Agricultural College at Lincoln in 1880, it has promoted a scientific approach to farming on the Canterbury Plains.

Exported initially to Britain, and later all around the world, lambs fattened on the Canterbury

Jet boating is an exhilerating activity for all the family.

Plains became known as 'Canterbury Lamb'. By carefully 'rotating' pasture and crops, Canterbury's farmers help maintain soil fertility. Legume crops, such as peas, add nitrogen to the soil, and save on expensive artificial fertilisers.

Canterbury's 'braided' rivers weave their way through wide beds of shingle as they cross the plains. Only in flood conditions does water stretch from bank to bank. The world-famous 'Hamilton Jet' was invented in Canterbury in the 1930s by Charles Hamilton. Without propellers, his jet boats were designed to operate in Canterbury's shallow, shifting rivers. They are now the basis for tourism operations on many rivers around the world.

Richard Pearse

Richard Pearse (1877-1953), a South Canterbury farmer, is believed by many to have been the first person to fly. Using a local road near Temuka as a runway, he took off in his homemade plane and flew for about 100 m. His flight, which came to a prickly end in a gorse bush, occurred nine months before the Wright brothers' first flight in America.

Methven

Methven is situated on the edge of the Canterbury Plains, only 25 km from Mount Hutt skifield. In summer it is a quiet farming town, but in winter it becomes a lively ski resort. Jet boating the Rakaia Gorge and hot-air ballooning now add to Methven's tourist appeal.

The countryside around Methven makes it ideal for hot-air ballooning.

SOUTH ISLAND

DID YOU KNOW?

- **Because of a shortage** of local timber on the Canterbury Plains, many early European settlers built 'cob' cottages. These 'mud huts' were built from rammed, but unfired, clay bricks. They lasted well in Canterbury's dry climate. Some still exist today.
- **Lake Ellesmere** is one of the South Island's most extensive lakes, but is less than 2 m deep. This swampy lake is a wetland nature reserve.
- **The highest temperature** ever recorded in New Zealand was 42.4 °C in February 1973, at Rangiora, near the northern end of the Canterbury Plains.
- **The Ashburton district** is known as the 'granary of New Zealand', thanks to its extensive fields of wheat and other grain crops.

Behind the Plains

Canterbury's 'downs' are in fact 'ups'! They are the gentle foothills of the Southern Alps, separating the plains from the mountains. Their gentle slopes are dotted by sheep, receive more rainfall and are cut occasionally by river gorges.

In summer, Peel Forest Park's trees and streams are a popular escape from the heat of the Canterbury Plains. These foothills of the Southern Alps provide relief from the straight lines of the plains!

SOUTH ISLAND

Christchurch – Mainland Capital

Shoppers and tourists walking through Christchurch's Cathedral Square are likely to be distracted by the oratory of one of Christchurch's living, and very eccentric, icons – the Wizard.

Christchurch's reputation for being 'more English than the English' may have been the intention of its founders in 1850, but it is not a reputation that many would agree with today, least of all its rugby supporters! Although it has retained some English characteristics, it is very much a New Zealand city.

Christ's College was founded at Lyttelton in 1851 by the chaplain of one of Canterbury's 'First Four Ships'. It was modelled on 'the great grammar schools of England'.

History

In 1850 Canterbury's 'First Four Ships' brought 782 carefully selected migrants from Britain to begin a new life at Christchurch. The new settlement was planned in England by the bishops and baronets of the Canterbury Association. It was intended to become a model English society, based on church attendance, education and agriculture.

Christchurch's Englishness is based on more than its old churches and schools. Cricket at Hagley Park and punting on the Avon keep true English traditions alive today.

Christchurch's first streets were laid out on a swampy site on the Canterbury Plains. It soon gained a reputation for bog, fog and mud. By the 1870s it was regarded as the unhealthiest town in the colony, with a death rate twice the national average.

Drains and sewers got rid of Christchurch's bog and mud, and an early programme of tree planting helped transform Christchurch into today's 'Garden City'.

On cold, calm, winter mornings Christchurch's fog mixes with smoke

QUICK FACTS:
- Christchurch (population 331,000) is New Zealand's third largest city.
- The Port Hills, Hagley Park and the Avon River are the main landmarks.
- Christchurch is the commercial, industrial and cultural centre of the Canterbury Plains.
- Christchurch's economy is based on processing agricultural products.

EVENTS CALENDAR:
January:
International Buskers Festival
July:
Hot-air Balloon Festival

One of the many beautiful gardens in Christchurch.

from coal fires and car exhausts to make an unhealthy smog.

Small 'English' farms were expected to provide for the first settlers' needs, but to begin with there was more interest in grazing sheep on the surrounding plains. Christchurch grew slowly until more intensive, mixed farming was established on the surrounding plains. Unlike Dunedin further south, it failed to benefit from the gold rushes of the 1860s and 1870s.

In the 1880s exports to Britain of frozen meat, 'Canterbury lamb', finally got Christchurch going. Processing of agricultural products is still the backbone of Christchurch's economy.

Out and about in Christchurch

Antarctic Centre: Christchurch is the gateway to the Antarctic, supplying both American and New Zealand bases on the icy continent. Robert Scott's ill-fated 1910 expedition, and Sir Edmund Hillary's successful 1958 expedition, both set off for the South Pole from Christchurch.

Multimedia presentations at the International Antarctic Centre, near Christchurch International Airport, tell the full story of Antarctica's environment and exploration.

Sport: Many rugby and cricket legends have been created on the turf of Lancaster Park. Sir Richard Hadlee, one of New Zealand's greatest cricket heroes, took many of his record-beating tally of 431 test wickets at Lancaster Park. Fervent rugby supporters, Cantabrians are renowned for the 'welcome' they give visiting teams!

Banks Peninsula

Named after Joseph Banks, Captain Cook's botanist, Banks Peninsula is an extinct volcano! Streams and waves have eroded deep sheltered gullies, which make excellent harbours.

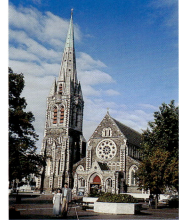

Christchurch, like its cathedral, took much longer to become well established than its founders had planned. The Cathedral, begun in 1864, took 37 years to complete.

Lyttelton: Christchurch's economy is dependent not only on the farms of the Canterbury Plains but also on the port of Lyttelton. With its excellent harbour, Lyttelton was the original site chosen for Christchurch, but its lack of flat land made it impractical. The first settlers had to make their way over the Port Hills to an alternative site. A road and rail tunnel under the Port Hills now links Lyttelton to Christchurch.

Akaroa: The quaint village of Akaroa is a reminder that New Zealand could have become a French colony and Christchurch could now be 'more French than the French'. In 1838 the captain of a French whaling boat bought land on Banks Peninsula, but a few months before the first French settlers arrived the Treaty of Waitangi was signed and New Zealand became a British colony. C'est la vie!

Hector's dolphin: The Banks Peninsula Marine Mammal Sanctuary protects the rare Hector's dolphin, which lives only in New Zealand seas. The survival of the species is threatened by fishing nets, pollution and collisions with boats.

SOUTH ISLAND

DID YOU KNOW?

- **Christchurch** was named after Christ Church College at Oxford University in England. The city's founders placed great importance on education.
- **Wilding Park**, the city's tennis centre, is named after Anthony Wilding (1883-1915), Christchurch's and New Zealand's greatest-ever tennis player. He won ten Wimbledon titles, four Davis Cups, and an Olympic bronze medal!
- **Of New Zealand's** four main cities, Christchurch was the first to install a sewerage system, but the last to install a city-wide water supply.
- **A cricket pavilion** built at Hagley Park in 1863 is New Zealand's oldest sports building.
- **Christchurch** claims to be capital of the Mainland! Well, it is the largest city of New Zealand's largest island. (The Mainland, also known as South Island, was once called Middle Island.)
- **Christchurch** hosted the Commonwealth Games in 1974. The Games are remembered for Dick Tayler's gold medal and John Walker's silver.

SOUTH ISLAND

Southern Alps – Crossing Over

The Southern Alps.

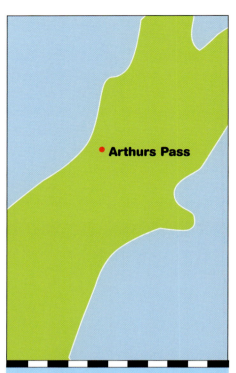

• Arthurs Pass

The Southern Alps form a rugged barrier, which people cross over for a variety of reasons. For pre-European Maori it was to trade greenstone; for the first Europeans it was to explore or find gold; for today's tourists and trampers it is to marvel at glaciers and fiords; for mountaineers and endurance athletes it is simply the challenge!

QUICK FACTS:

- Several Maori greenstone trails crossed over the Southern Alps.
- There are four road passes over the Main Divide.
- Two tunnels (one road, one rail) cut through the Southern Alps.
- Some people still prefer to cross the Main Divide on foot.
- Competitors in the 'Coast to Coast' race cycle, run and kayak their way over the Southern Alps.

Maori crossings

Long before Europeans arrived in New Zealand, West Coast Maori pioneered trails across the Southern Alps. They had to cross the 'Main Divide' to trade their valuable greenstone with other tribes throughout New Zealand. Greenstone was valued by Maori as a superior woodworking tool, and for its ornamental qualities.

Climbing over high mountain passes presented a significant challenge, even in summer. Flax sandals and cloaks provided little protection from the rocks and the cold. Fern roots and other vegetables were taken with them and eels and birds were trapped along the way. Slaves, taken to carry the heavy greenstone, sometimes became part of the traders' diet when food supplies ran low.

Greenstone trails allowed greenstone to be traded beyond the West Coast, but they also allowed enemy tribes to get in. Ngati Warangi's greenstone trade with Ngai Tahu ended when Ngai Tahu attacked over the Browning Pass and claimed the greenstone source for themselves.

The annual 'Coast to Coast' race is not the quickest way over the Southern Alps but it is certainly the most tiring! The fastest competitors cycle, run and kayak the 239 km from Kumara Beach on the West Coast to Sumner Beach, Christchurch in less than twelve hours.

European explorers

In the 1850s and 1860s European explorers followed in the footsteps of Maori greenstone traders. They had better equipment but did not have the ability of the Maori to live off the land. Many explorers took local Maori guides with them.

The naming of the passes across the Main Divide does seem to have been a little unfair at times.

- Harper's Pass is named after the first European explorer to cross it, not the Maori guide who led him there!
- Whitcombe Pass, an old Maori greenstone trail, was not named

after John Baker and Samuel Butler who in 1861 were the first Europeans to find it. It was named after another European who crossed over the pass some time later and drowned in the Taramakau River.
• In 1863 Charles Cameron, a gold prospector, became the first European to cross the Haast Pass. But it was the better known Julius von Haast, who crossed over soon after him, that the pass is named after.
• Arthurs Pass was named after Arthur Dobson in 1864. Dobson had been told about the pass by Tarapuhi, a local Maori chief.

Crossing over by road

The **Arthurs Pass** road was the first, and still the highest, road across the Southern Alps. It was built in 1865-66 in a desperate bid by Christchurch to profit from the West Coast's gold rush. A coach road was hurriedly constructed over Arthurs Pass (altitude 924 m). West Coasters, angry at having to pay for a road they didn't want, continued to ship their golden fortunes to Nelson.

Haast Pass (altitude 563 m) is the second lowest road pass across the Main Divide, and was the most difficult to build. Begun in 1929, it was completed 36 years later at a cost of $11 million! Today it is a popular tourist road, which leads from Wanaka and Queenstown to the glaciers and forests of Westland's World Heritage Area.

Lewis Pass is New Zealand's second highest road pass, reaching an altitude of 912 m. The road was built in 1937, linking Christchurch to Westport. Although it was used by Maori as a greenstone trail it wasn't used during the nineteenth century gold rushes.

Crossing over by rail

The Otira Tunnel has a gradient of 1:33, is 8.6 km long and took fifteen years to complete. When it was finished in 1923 it put the old Cobb & Co coaches out of business. Today it is used by trains railing out West Coast Coal and carrying day-tripping tourists on a scenic ride from Christchurch to Greymouth.

SOUTH ISLAND

DID YOU KNOW?

• The **'Main Divide'** is the highest ridgeline separating rivers flowing to the Tasman Sea from those flowing to the Pacific Ocean.
• **In 1836** Te Puoho and his band of Ngati Toa warriors crossed an old Maori greenstone trail (now called Haast Pass) to launch a surprise 'back door' attack on Ngai Tahu near Lake Wanaka.
• **The most popular walk** over the Main Divide is the 36 km Routeburn Track. Over 10,000 people walk the track each year. Three-quarters of them are from outside New Zealand. The Harris Saddle (1278 m), which is the actual divide, was first crossed by a European in 1863.
• **The southernmost** and lowest road crossing of the South Island's mountain backbone is at 'The Divide' (532 m) on the road to Milford Sound. Getting the road to The Divide was the easy bit – the Homer Tunnel had to be blasted through before it reached Milford Sound!
• **The road** through Porters Pass (near Arthurs Pass) is about 20 m higher than Arthurs Pass, but it is not actually on the Main Divide.

Back to basics

For experienced climbers and trampers the Copland Track in Westland National Park is a popular route over the Main Divide. Full alpine equipment, and usually an experienced guide, are required to get over the snow-and ice-covered Copland Pass. From there it is a steep descent to the Hermitage at Mount Cook.

SOUTH ISLAND

Southern Alps - High Country

Canterbury's legendary high country sheep stations are tucked between soaring, snow-covered peaks, far from the open plains to the east. Falling wool prices, serious soil erosion and fences now keep most sheep down off the highest slopes, but annual mustering still gathers sheep from vast areas of difficult terrain.

The Southern Alps, the South Island's mountain backbone, stretches nearly the full length of the island. From early European sheep farmers to modern mountaineers and skiers, the Southern Alps have proved to be an irresistible attraction.

QUICK FACTS:
- Mount Cook (3754 m) is New Zealand's highest mountain.
- There are nineteen peaks in the South Island over 3000 m high.
- Tasman Glacier (29 km) is New Zealand's longest glacier.
- The New Zealand Government owns most of the South Island high country.

Sheep station legends

Among the first to exploit the deep valleys and tussock-covered slopes of the Southern Alps was Samuel Butler. Arriving in New Zealand in 1860, he soon leased huge 'runs' at the head of the Rangitata River and stocked them with merino sheep (right). After four years Butler sold his 'Mesopotamia' sheep run and returned to England with a handsome profit. Over the next hundred years the hard and lonely lifestyle of remote, high country sheep farmers and their families has become part of New Zealand folklore. Butler's classic 1873 novel, *Erewhon*, is based on his brief high country experiences in New Zealand.

'Fenced in' by snow above, rivers below and chasms on either side, the sheep were left to graze the high

tussock slopes. The sheep were mustered (gathered together) for shearing and to spend the winters on the more sheltered river-flats. Dogs and horses were vital for working sheep in this mountainous landscape. Often cut off for weeks on end by snow and floods, the high country sheep farmers had little contact with the outside world.

High country stations today

Now called 'stations', the huge sheep runs are undergoing dramatic changes. If *Erewhon* symbolises the start of New Zealand's high country sheep farming, Molesworth (once the largest sheep station in the country) signalled its decline. Since 1949, when Molesworth was finally abandoned by sheep farmers, the steep and fragile slopes of the Southern Alps have increasingly been fenced off and 'retired' from grazing.

Delicate mountain slopes and soils have been devastated by over a century of tussock burning (to promote tender new shoots for sheep to graze on), overgrazing by sheep and the introduction of deer and rabbits.

Rabbits had become widespread in New Zealand by the 1840s. Breeding rapidly and estimated to eat six times more grass than a sheep, they put many high country sheep farmers out of business in the 1880s. The rabbit plague was not brought under some kind of control until the 1950s, but rabbits were rampant again by the 1980s. The controversial release of the rabbit-killing calicivirus in the 1990s may not provide a final solution to the rabbit problem. By the 1990s about one sixth of the South Island was owned by the government and leased to high country farmers. Farmers are now being encouraged to give up their leases on higher mountain slopes in return for ownership of their more productive river-flats.

Extensive sheep farming will always be part of the heritage of the Southern Alps, but a more sustainable future is now emerging. It will be based on more intensive farming on improved river-flat pastures, and the conservation and recreational use of the tussocked upper slopes.

Mount Cook National Park is one of several parks that preserve the natural landscapes of the Southern Alps. Its spectacular scenery and alpine wilderness attract tourists, climbers, trampers and skiers from around the world. The National Park was established in 1953, the year Sir Edmund Hillary climbed Everest. In 1990 it became a World Heritage Area. The Park's Tasman Glacier (29 km) is New Zealand's longest glacier.

Recreation in the mountains

Hunting: Deer were introduced by early European settlers for recreational hunting purposes. Thriving here they added to the destruction of forests and erosion of soil in the mountains. Their hunting today is both for recreational and pest control purposes.

Climbing: Known as Aoraki (cloud-piercer) to Maori, Mount Cook was first climbed on Christmas Day, 1894, by three New Zealanders, Fyfe, Graham and Clark. Today, the challenge of New Zealand's highest peaks and the skill of its leading climbers are admired around the world.

Tramping: The mountains of the Southern Alps, with their national and forest parks, network of tracks and huts and outstanding scenery, have earned New Zealand the reputation of being a tramper's (walker's) paradise.

Skiing: There are nineteen skifields in the mountains of the South Island, from Rainbow in the north to the Remarkables in the south. Glacier skiing on the Tasman Glacier, 'Nordic' (cross-country) skiing near Cardrona and heli-skiing in remote high country basins are also available.

SOUTH ISLAND

DID YOU KNOW?

- **According to** the New Zealand Geographic Board, the Southern Alps extend from Mount Aspiring in the south to Lewis Pass in the north, a distance of nearly 370 km. Popular use of the term 'Southern Alps' often refers to the full length of New Zealand's mountain backbone, from Fiordland to the Kaikoura Ranges.
- **Erewhon**, the name of Samuel Butler's classic high country novel, is (with one small change) 'nowhere' spelt backwards. It reflects the isolation of the sheep run he established in the 1860s. Butler's original sheep run was called Mesopotamia (between two rivers). Today's Erewhon Station, only a part of that original run, now raises cattle and deer as well as merino sheep.
- **Mount Hutt**, near Methven, has the longest ski season of all New Zealand's skifields.
- **The Tasman Glacier** offers skiers a continuous downhill run of 12 km.
- **In 1948** Sir Edmund Hillary was a member of the first group to climb Mount Cook via the South Ridge.
- **There are over 350 glaciers** in the mountains of the South Island, some reaching closer to the sea than any other glaciers at a similar latitude anywhere else in the world.

OTHER ISLANDS

Across the water – Island Lifestyles

Nearly 1000 people commute daily to school and office in Auckland.

New Zealand is made up of about 600 islands, from Raoul Island in the north to Campbell Island in the south. Most are rarely seen or heard of, several are important nature reserves and only Stewart Island, Chatham Islands, Great Barrier Island and Waiheke Island have significant resident populations.

Waiheke Island

Waiheke Island, with over 6000 permanent residents, is New Zealand's most populated offshore island. Not all that long ago it was a quiet retreat for alternative lifestylers – 'refugees' from suburban Auckland. Now that it is only minutes away from downtown Auckland by fast ferry, western Waiheke has itself become an Auckland suburb. Oneroa is the island's main 'urban' centre.

Waiheke's unspoilt beaches and extra sunshine make stepping off the island's commuter ferry feel like going on holiday. Much of eastern Waiheke is still bush and farmland providing an even more peaceful retreat from downtown Oneroa!

Waiheke's vineyards have a fine reputation. The grapes benefit from Waiheke's mild temperatures and extra sunshine.

Waiheke's best beaches face away from Auckland out into the Hauraki Gulf.

Great Barrier Island

Great and Little Barrier islands were named by Captain Cook for the way they shelter the Hauraki Gulf from easterly swells and storms. Great Barrier, the larger of the two islands, was known to Maori as Aotea. About 90 km from Auckland, Great Barrier is now home to a little over 1000 people.

Geologically and scenically, Great Barrier has much in common with the Coromandel Peninsula, only a short hop across the Colville Channel. Early European interest was based on whaling, kauri logging and mining of gold, silver and copper.

For a while Great Barrier had a reputation for its communes, hippies and hermits and it still does attract those who want to 'get away from the world'. There are few opportunities for

QUICK FACTS:
- Stewart Island is New Zealand's largest offshore island.
- Great Barrier Island is the North Island's largest offshore island.
- Waiheke is New Zealand's most populated offshore island.
- New Zealand's most remote community lives in the Chatham Islands.

EVENTS CALENDAR:
January:
Longboard Classic Surfing Contest, Great Barrier Island
April:
Easter Jazz Festival, Waiheke Island
Muttonbird season opens on Stewart Island

full-time employment on the island today, but a living can be made by those who are independent, thrifty, creative and adaptable.

Tourist interest in 'the Barrier' has increased as ferry and plane services have improved over the years. Today the island is only half an hour by plane, or one-and-a-half hours by fast ferry, from Auckland. After the hectic summer invasion of holidaymakers the pace of life subsides and the locals get the island back to themselves.

Visitors are attracted by the island's scenery – rugged mountains, regenerating bush, beautiful beaches and hot springs – and excellent fishing and diving. With about one third of the island already owned by the Government there is increasing pressure to preserve the island's natural heritage by creating a Great Barrier National Park.

Stewart Island

Stewart Island, separated from the mainland by Foveaux Strait, is New Zealand's third largest island. It was inhabited by Maori from the thirteenth century.

European sealers and whalers established small coastal settlements early in the nineteenth century. Fishing, logging and sawmilling and mining of gold and tin followed, but only the fishing has remained. Today a small fishing fleet and tourism sustain the island's economy and its 400 permanent residents. Regular flights from Invercargill and a ferry service from Bluff transport visitors across Foveaux Strait.

Maori called Stewart Island Rakiura (glowing sky) because of its rich sunsets and the spectacular 'southern lights' (aurora australis). Europeans called it both South Island and New Leinster before naming it after William Stewart, the first officer of a sealing ship that visited the island in 1809.

Few Maori ever lived permanently on Stewart Island but many visited it each year to catch titi ('muttonbirds' or sooty shearwaters). The traditional custom of muttonbirding still continues today.

Energetic trampers, and those looking for peaceful relaxation, are drawn to the tranquil beauty of Stewart Island. Stewart Island is a likely candidate for New Zealand's next national park.

The island is home to the Southern tokoeka kiwi which, unlike other species of kiwi, is active in daylight hours. Stewart Island, with few predators, is one place that kiwi populations are not threatened.

Chatham Islands

Over 700 people live in the Chatham Islands, New Zealand's most remote community, 860 km east of Christchurch. Lying only a few degrees from the international dateline, the Chatham Islands were one of the first places in the world to welcome the start of the third millennium. Tiny South East Island is New Zealand's most easterly point.

The Islands' original settlers were Polynesians known as Moriori. They were virtually trapped on their islands by a shortage of timber for making ocean-going boats until their discovery in 1791.

Tommy Solomon, thought to have been the last full-blooded Moriori, died in 1933. The Moriori were almost wiped out by an invasion of mainland Maori in 1835. Today nearly two-thirds of the population is of mainland Maori descent.

Most Chatham Islanders make a hard-earned living from their isolated and windswept home by fishing and farming. Their produce is sold in mainland markets.

OTHER ISLANDS

DID YOU KNOW?

- **New Zealand** was once known for its three islands – North Island, Middle Island (now South Island) and South Island (now Stewart Island).
- **Waiheke's** population swells from about 6000 to an estimated 20,000 during the January holiday season. Frequent summer water shortages are not surprising!
- **In 1998** around 325,000 people visited Waiheke Island, two-thirds of them day-trippers from Auckland.
- **Great Barrier Island** has no mains electricity. Gradually the throb of diesel generators at dawn and dusk is being replaced by silent solar and wind energy sources.
- **Great Barrier Island** has no possums! It is the largest possum-free area in New Zealand.
- **Great Barrier** claims the last whaling station built in New Zealand (1957), and the world's first airmail postal service (1897) – pigeon post to the mainland! A service still operates today.
- **When Captain Cook** sailed past Stewart Island in 1770 he thought it was attached to the mainland. He called it Cape South and showed it on his maps as a peninsula. His mistake wasn't corrected for about another 40 years.
- **According to Maori legend** Stewart Island was the anchor that held Maui's canoe (the South Island) while he fished the North Island out of the sea.
- **The Chatham Islands** are linked to the South Island by an undersea ridge called the Chatham Rise.
- **The Chatham Islands**, New Zealand's most easterly land, actually lie in the western hemisphere. Work that one out!

OTHER ISLANDS

Across the water – Natural Sanctuaries

Tiritiri Matangi lies 4 km from the mainland in Auckland's Hauraki Gulf. Once farmed, the island has been cleared of rats and other predators and is being replanted in native trees. Many endangered bird species have been introduced to the island, including takahe from Fiordland. The island is an 'open' sanctuary. Visitors are welcomed but pets are not allowed and visitors are asked to ensure they do not introduce rats or start fires.

At the end of the last ice age ice caps melted and the sea level rose, trapping flora and fauna on offshore islands. Some species were wiped out on the mainland by the impact of humans and survived only on the more remote offshore islands. If it were not for these 'living museums', many more New Zealand species would have become extinct.

New Zealand's offshore islands continue to play a vital role in the conservation of its native plants and animals. Once cleared of introduced animals, an increasing number of islands provide safe havens for some of New Zealand's most endangered species.

Department of Conservation

The Department of Conservation (DoC) manages over 200 of New Zealand's islands. Nearly half these islands are nature reserves and permits are required for visits.

Poor Knights Islands

The Poor Knights Islands provide sanctuary to flora and fauna both above and below sea level. Its marine reserve (established in 1981) protects the rare sponges and fish found in its subtropical waters. On land it has a healthy population of tuatara, New Zealand's 'living fossil' and the world's only surviving link with ancient dinosaurs; the rest of its beak-headed family have been extinct for 100 million years! The tuatara no longer survives in the wild on the mainland.

Little Barrier Island

Little Barrier Island is considered to be one of the world's most important nature reserves. It has the only rainforests in New Zealand that have been unaffected by people, deer or possums. Since the eradication of feral cats in 1980 it has provided a sanctuary for a variety of endangered species, including the kokako, stitchbird (left) and kakapo.

Kapiti Island

Once a stronghold for Maori tribes, Kapiti Island now protects some of New Zealand's most threatened birds, including takahe, kokako, kiwi and stitchbirds. Established in 1897, it was one of New Zealand's first forest and bird sanctuaries. The island lies 6 km offshore from Waikanae, on the North Island's lower west coast. Marine sanctuaries have also been established around its shores.

QUICK FACTS:
- Forty-four bird species have become extinct in New Zealand since humans arrived.
- Some threatened species survive only on offshore islands.
- Offshore islands play an important role in preserving threatened species.
- About one sixth of New Zealand's offshore islands are nature reserves.

Stephens Island

Stephens Island, at the northern tip of the Marlborough Sounds, is the home of New Zealand's rarest frog. Hamilton's frog, found only on Stephens and Maud islands (see below), lives in a dry environment and gets wet only when it rains! The frogs share the island, now a nature reserve, with a population of tuatara (above).

Maud Island

Sheltered by the Marlborough Sounds, Maud Island is best known for its population of kakapo, New Zealand's flightless parrot. As well as being the world's largest parrot it is also one of the world's most threatened birds. Kakapo were introduced to the sanctuary of predator-free Maud Island from Fiordland and Stewart Island in an attempt to establish a breeding colony and save the species from extinction.

Outlying islands

About 5 per cent of New Zealand's islands lie well beyond its shores and were never part of its mainland. These islands, from subtropical Raoul Island in the north to subantarctic Campbell Island in the south and the Chathams in the east, all have conservation stories to tell.

Kermadec Islands

The Kermadecs lie 1000 km northeast of Auckland, at about 30° south of the equator. Named after their French discoverers, the islands were annexed by New Zealand in 1887. Since then the introduction of fire, rats, goats and cats has destroyed much of the islands' natural environment. Only the Meyer Islands escaped the introduction of predators. Still in their original condition, they are teeming with bird life. The only inhabitants today are visiting New Zealand research scientists based on volcanic Raoul Island. The eradication of pests has begun and the goats have gone.

Chatham Islands

In 1976 the last seven Chatham Island robins in the world were rescued from their dying forest habitat on Little Mangere Island and transferred to regenerating bush on nearby Mangere Island. It was a final and desperate effort to save the species from extinction. To increase their breeding rate eggs from the last two females were placed in the nests of Chatham Island tits. With the help of these 'foster' parents the species was miraculously brought back from the brink of extinction. By 2000 the number of robins had increased to over 200.

Auckland Islands

The windswept Auckland Islands are 320 km south of Stewart Island, well on the way to Antarctica. They are best known for the shipwreck of the *General Grant* and its cargo of gold in 1866. Five survivors were rescued eighteen months later. They managed to light a fire with their last match and kept it going for eighteen months! One of the survivors was killed three years later trying to salvage the sunken gold.

OTHER ISLANDS

DID YOU KNOW?

- **Tuatara** can live up to 100 years but need an environment free of rats and other predators to survive.
- **Cats** had been introduced to Little Barrier Island by the 1870s and for 100 years the island had an estimated feral cat population of 800. A cat eradication programme began in 1977 and by 1980 they were all gone.
- **Quarantine Island** (Otago Harbour) was first used as a defence against exotic diseases in 1863 when a case of smallpox was found on a migrant ship. To prevent the disease spreading, the 400 new settlers on board were quarantined on the island for five weeks. Somes Island (Wellington) and Quail Island (Lyttelton) were once used in a similar way.

AMAZING NEW ZEALAND QUIZ

1. **New Zealand has had three different capital cities at different times in its short history.**
   - Can you name all three?
   - Can you name them all in the right order?

2. **Which New Zealand towns would you visit to see:**
   - a kumara festival?
   - a kiwifruit festival?
   - a wild foods festival?

3. **New Zealand has a colourful gold-mining history.**
   - Name two towns in the North Island that were important gold-mining centres.
   - Which one is named after a ship used to export kauri spars?
   - Which South Island region had a gold rush in 1863 and what percentage of the European population moved there as a result?

4. **Which North Island town's local college offers a surfing academy for international students?**

5. **Who is Tane Mahuta, how old is he, how tall is he and where does he live?**

6. **Which New Zealand city is built over and around 48 volcanoes, and what is the name of its youngest and biggest volcano?**

7. **Which New Zealand towns or cities could you visit if you wanted to:**
   - go hot air ballooning?
   - go black-water rafting, abseiling and pot-holing, and see glow-worms?
   - go whale-watching?

8. **Because New Zealand is on the Pacific Rim of Fire, it is prone to earthquakes.**
   - Name a fatal earthquake in the North Island. When did it happen and how many people were killed?
   - Name another fatal earthquake in the South Island. When did it happen and how many people were killed?

9. **Who was Tutanekai and what musical instrument did he play? What did his lover do that made her famous?**

10. **According to Maori legend, who died because he bit off more than he could chew?**

11. **Which New Zealand city sits on three major fault lines and what did this have to do with Bill Robinson?**

12. **If you lived in Colliers Creek, Westland, what would you remember most about January 1994?**

13. **New Zealand has some unique wildlife. Can you name these 'kiwis'?**
    - The world's largest parrot
    - The world's last living member of the dinosaur family
    - A rare dolphin that only lives in New Zealand waters

14 Captain Cook features in the history of almost every region in New Zealand.
- Where was he when he was feeling doubtful?
- Where was he when he wrote about fertile and well-inhabited land?
- Where was he when he made a mistake about an area with a beautiful climate and fertile plains?

15 New Zealand is famous for its fruit and vegetables, and some giant roadside attractions celebrate local produce.
- Where would you find a giant kiwifruit?
- Where would you find a giant apple and pear?

16 New Zealanders take part in a wide variety of sports, some well known, others not so well known. Where would you go to see people compete in the these events?
- World Stone Sawing Championships
- Golden Axe
- A kilikiti tournamant
- Miners' Stampede wheelbarrow race

17 Why did teachers at Edgecumbe College in the Bay of Plenty evacuate their classrooms at 1.35 p.m. on 2 March 1987? Why was it a good thing that they did?

18 New Zealand has had a history of mining for gold, coal and sulphur. Where did the following mining disasters happen and what were the miners mining for at the time?
- 1914; mine destroyed on an off shore island, killing twelve miners
- 1896; a mining disaster killed 65 miners
- 1967; an explosion in a mine killed nineteen miners

19 Which seabirds can circumnavigate the globe without once setting foot on land? Which South Island city has a colony of these amazing birds on its doorstep?

20 Which famous warrior chief met King George IV in London and helped write a Maori dictionary?

Answers:
1. Russell, Auckland, Wellington
2. Dargaville, Te Puke, Hokitika
3. Any two of: Coromandel; Thames, Waihi; Coromandel; West Coast, 10 per cent
4. Raglan
5. A giant kauri, 1200 years old, 50 m tall, in the Waipoua Forest
6. Auckland, Rangitoto
7. Hamilton, Waitomo, Kaikoura
8. North Island: Hawkes Bay earthquake, 1931, 256 people. South Island: either Murchison earthquake, 1929, 17 people or Inangahua earthquake, 1968, 2 people
9. A Maori warrior who lived on Mokoia Island in Lake Rotorua, he played the flute. She swam out to the island.
10. Te Mata.
11. Wellington, he designed a way to help buildings withstand earthquakes, called base isolation.
12. It was the month when they had the rainiest day in New Zealand history, when 682 mm of rain was recorded.
13. Kakapo, tuatara, Hector's dolphin
14. Doubtful Sound in Fiordland, the Bay of Plenty, Poverty Bay
15. Te Puke, Cromwell
16. Oamaru, Tokoroa, Auckland, Waihi
17. Because there had just been a small earthquake, and it was followed by a major earthquake.
18. White Island, sulphur; Brunner Mine, coal; Strongman Mine, coal.
19. Royal albatross, Dunedin.
20. Hongi Hika.

INDEX

A
Abel Tasman National Park 47
Akaroa 66, 67
Albany 15
Alexandra 58, 59
Antarctic, Antarctica, Antarctic Centre 67, 75
Aotearoa 10
Apirana Ngata, Sir 29
Arrowtown 58
Arthurs Pass 68, 69
Ashburton 64, 65
Atiamuri 25
Auckland, Auckland City 7, 8, 10, 11, 12, 14-19, 20, 22, 45, 72, 73, 74, 75
Auckland Domain 16
Auckland Harbour Bridge 15
Auckland Islands 75
Auckland, South 19
Avon River 66

B
Balclutha 56
Banks Peninsula 67
Banks Peninsula Marine Mammals Sanctuary 67
Bay of Islands 7, 8, 10, 11, 12, 13,
Bay of Plenty 8, 26-27, 32
Birkenhead 16
Blackball 49
Blenheim 46, 47
Bluff 54, 55, 73
Browning Pass 68
Buller Gorge 48
Buller River 48, 50
Bulls 40, 41

C
Cambridge 22
Campbell Island 72, 75
Canterbury 8
Canterbury Plains 41, 64-65
Cape Brett 13
Cape Colville 20
Cape Farewell 47
Cape Kidnappers 31
Cape Reinga 12
Cardrona 59, 61, 71
Cathedral Caves 55
Catlins Coast 55
Central Otago 56, 58-59
Chateau, The 37
Chatham Islands 29, 72, 73, 75
Christchurch 7, 64, 66-67, 68, 69, 73
Clutha River 59
Clyde Dam 58, 59
Cook Strait 7, 45, 50
Cook Strait ferry 7, 42, 47
Cornwall Park 17
Coromandel, Coromandel Peninsula 20-21, 72

Coronet Peak 61
Crater Lake 37
Cromwell 58, 59
Crown range 61
Curio Bay 55

D
Dargaville 12, 13
Doubtful Sound 52
Drury 15
Dunedin 7, 56-57, 67

E
East Cape 28-29
East Tamaki 15
Eden Park 19
Edendale 55
Edinburgh 56, 57
Egmont National Park 39
Emerald Lakes 37

F
Fairlie 62
Farewell Spit 47
Fiordland 51, 52-53, 71, 74, 75
Fiordland National Park 52, 54
Foveaux Strait 55, 73
Fox, Fox Glacier 49, 50, 51
Franz Josef, Franz Josef Glacier 49, 50, 51

G
Gisborne 8, 27, 28, 29, 31
Golden Bay 46, 47
Gondwanaland 6, 12
Gore 54, 55
Great Barrier Island 14, 72, 73
Greymouth 48, 49, 69

H
Haast Pass 68
Hagley Park 66
Hamilton 22, 25
Harpers Pass 68
Hastings 30, 31
Hauraki Gulf 15, 72, 74
Havelock 46
Havelock North 31
Hawaii 19
Hawera 38
Hawke Bay 31
Hawke's Bay 7, 8, 30-31
Heaphy Track 47
Helensville 13
Heretaunga Plains 30
Hermitage 69
Hokianga Harbour 10
Hokianga sandhills 13
Hokitika 48, 49
Hokonui 54
Homer Tunnel 53, 69
Hot Water Beach 21
Huka Falls 25
Huntly 23, 24, 25

I
Inangahua 50, 51
Invercargill 54, 55, 60

K
Kahurangi National Park 47
Kaikoura 46, 47
Kaikoura Ranges 71
Kaingaroa Forest 32, 33
Kaipara Harbour 12, 13
Kapiti Island 74
Kapuni gas field 39
Karapiro (see Lake Karapiro)
Katikati 27
Kauaeranga Valley 21
Kauri Coast 13
Kawarau River 58, 61
Kawerau 26, 27
Kawerau River 27
Kemp House 10
Kerikeri 10, 11, 13
Kermadec Islands 75
Ketetahi Springs 37
King Country 22, 24
Kingston 60, 61
Kororareka 11
Kumara Beach

L
Lake Benmore 63
Lake Dunstan 59
Lake Ellesmere 65
Lake Grassmere 46
Lake Hawea 58
Lake Karapiro 24, 25
Lake Manapouri 53
Lake Matheson 48
Lake Ohakuri 25
Lake Ohau 63
Lake Pukaki 63
Lake Pupuke 16
Lake Quill 52
Lake Rotoiti (North Island) 35
Lake Rotoiti (South Island) 47
Lake Rotorua (North Island) 34,
Lake Rotoroa (South Island) 47
Lake Taupo 24, 25, 33, 34, 35, 38, 40
Lake Te Anau 53
Lake Tekapo 62, 63
Lake Wakatipu 58, 60, 61
Lake Wanaka 58, 69
Lancaster Park 67
Larnach Castle 56
Lewis Pass 69, 71
Lincoln 65
Little Barrier Island 14, 72, 74, 75
Little Mangere Island 75
Long Bay 15, 19
Lyttelton 66, 67, 75

M
Mackenzie country 62-63
Mackinnon Pass 53
Macraes Flat 57

Mahia Peninsula 28, 29
Makatote Viaduct 37
Maketu 27
Manapouri 52, 53
Manapouri Power Station 53, 55
Manawatu 8, 40-41
Mangere Island 75
Manukau City 15
Marlborough 8, 46-47
Marlborough Sounds, Maritime Park 46, 47, 75
Marsden Point 13
Matakoe Kauri Museum 13
Mataura River 55
Matauri Bay 13
Maud Island 75
Maui gas field 39
Maungakiekie (see One Tree Hill) 16, 17
Maungapohatu 29
Maungarei (see Mount Wellington) 15, 16, 17
Maungawhau (see Mount Eden) 14, 16, 17
Meola Reef 16, 17
Mercury Bay 21
Mercury Islands 21
Methven 64, 65, 71
Meyer Islands 75
Milford Sound 50, 52, 53, 69
Milford Track 52, 53
Mitre Peak 52
Moehau 20, 21
Moeraki 56, 57
Mokoia Island 33
Molesworth 70
Mossburn 55
Motonui 39
Motueka 46
Motuora 39
Mount Aspiring 71
Mount Aspiring National Park 59, 71
Mount Cook (Aoraki) 50, 63, 69, 70, 71
Mount Cook National Park 71
Mount Eden (see Maungawhau) 17
Mount Edgecumbe 26, 27
Mount Fuji 39
Mount Hikurangi 28
Mount Hobson 16
Mount Hutt 65, 70, 71
Mount John 63
Mount Maunganui 26, 27
Mount Ngauruhoe 35, 36, 37
Mount Pihanga 38
Mount Roskill 16
Mount Ruapehu 24, 32, 33, 35, 36, 37, 38, 40
Mount Taranaki 38, 39
Mount Tarawera 34, 35
Mount Tongariro 32, 35, 36, 37
Mount Victoria 45
Mount Wellington (see

78

Maungarei) 15, 16, 17
Moutua Gardens 41
Murchison 50
Murchison Mountains 53
Mystery Creek 22, 23

N
Napier 30, 31, 46-47
Naseby 58, 59
Nelson 7, 42, 51, 69
Nelson Lakes National Park 47
Nettlebed Cave 47
New Plymouth 7, 38, 39
Ngaruawahia 24
Ngauruhoe (see Mount Ngauruhoe)
Ninety Mile Beach 12, 13
Niue 18, 19
North Head 17
North Island 8, 10-45
North Shore City 15
Northland 8, 10-13
Norway 52
Nuku'alofa 19

O
Oamaru 56, 57
Ohakune 33, 36, 37
Ohinemutu 35
Okataina 32
Omarama 63
Onehunga 15
One Tree Hill (see Maungakiekie) 14, 16, 17
One Tree Hill Domain 17
Oneroa 72
Opotiki 26, 28
Orakei Korako 25
Oriental Bay 43
Otago 8, 56-59
Otago Peninsula 57
Otara 19
Otira Tunnel 69
Oturehua 58

P
Pacific Ocean 8
Palmerston North 40, 41, 47
Pancake Rocks (see Punakaiki)
Paparoa National Park 49
Parihaka 38
Peel Forest Park 65
Pelorus Sound 47
Penrose 15
Percy Burn 55
Picton 42, 46, 47
Piercy Island 13
Pink and White Terraces 35
Pohutu Geyser 34
Point Chevalier 16
Polynesia 6, 18, 19
Poor Knights Islands 74
Port Hills 66, 67
Port Nelson 46
Port Waikato 24

Porters Pass 69
Poverty Bay 27, 28, 29
Pukerangi 57
Punakaiki 49

Q
Quail Island 75
Quarantine Island 75
Queenstown 58, 59, 60-61, 69, 71

R
Raglan 22, 23
Rakaia Gorge 65
Rangiora 64, 65
Rangipo Desert 37
Rangipo power station 33
Rangiriri pa 22
Rangitaiki Plain 27
Rangitaiki River 27
Rangitata River 70
Rangitoto Island 14, 15, 16, 17
Raoul Island 72, 75
Raukumara Range 28
Raurimu, Raurimu Spiral 37
Red Crater 37
Reefton 49
Rees-Dart Track 71
Remarkables, Remarkable Range 61
Richmond 46
Ross 49
Rotoiti, North Island (see Lake Rotoiti)
Rotorua 32, 33, 34-35
Rotowaro 23
Routeburn Track 53, 69
Roxburgh Dam 59
Ruapehu (see Mount Ruapehu)
Ruapekepeka pa 11
Ruatoria 28, 29
Russell 10, 11, 12, 14

S
Shotover River 58, 61
Somes Island 75
South East Island 73
South Island 8, 11, 46-71
South Pole 67
Southern Alps 7, 49, 63, 64, 65, 68-69
Southland 8, 54
St Arnaud 47
Stephens Island 75
Stewart Island 8, 72, 73, 74
Stone Store, the 10
Sumner Beach 68
Sutherland, Donald 52
Sutherland Falls 52

T
Taharoa 23
Tahiti 19
Taiaroa Head 56, 57
Taieri Gorge Railway 57
Takaka 47

Tangiwai 37
Taramakau River 68
Taranaki 8, 38-39
Taranaki Falls 37
Tasman, Abel 6, 13, 47
Tasman Glacier 70, 71
Tasman Sea 7, 8, 24, 25, 49, 69
Tasmania 35
Taupiri 24
Taupo 22, 25, 32, 34-35
Taupo volcano 32
Tauranga 26, 27, 29, 31
Te Anau 52, 53
Te Araroa 29
Te Mata Peak 31
Te Papa Tongarewa 42, 43
Te Puke 26
Te Rauparaha 47
Te Wahi Pounamu (see World Heritage Area)
Te Wairoa 34
Temuka 65
Thames 20, 21, 25
Timaru 64
Tiritiri Matangi 74
Tiwai Point 54, 55
Tokaanu power station 33
Tokomaru Bay 28
Tokoroa 22, 32, 33
Tolaga Bay 28, 29
Tongariro (see Mount Tongariro)
Tongariro Hydroelectric Power Scheme 33
Tongariro National Park 22, 24, 33, 35, 36-37
Tongariro River 25, 35
Treble Cone 59
Tuakau 24, 25
Tuatapere 54, 55
Turangawaewae 24
Turangi 32, 33, 35
Turoa 36, 37
Twizel 62

U
Urewera 28, 29

V
Volcanic Plateau 32-33

W
Waiau River 55
Waiheke Island 72, 73
Waihi 20, 21
Waihi Beach 26
Waiho River 51
Waikanae 74
Waikato 8, 22-25,
Waikato River 23, 24-25, 40
Waimate North 11
Waiotapu 35
Waipiro Bay 29
Waipoua Forest 13
Waipu 13
Wairakei,

Wairakei power station 33
Wairau Valley 47
Wairoa 28, 30
Waitakere City 15
Waitakere Ranges 15
Waitaki Dam 63
Waitaki River 63
Waitangi 10, 11, 13
Waitangi National Reserve 11, 12,
Waitangi, Treaty of 7, 10, 11, 14, 41, 42, 43, 67
Waitara 38, 39
Waitemata Harbour 14, 15, 16, 17, 19
Waitomo Caves 23
Wanaka 58, 59, 61, 69
Wanganui 7, 8, 40, 41, 42
Wellington 7, 8, 15, 19, 42-45, 47, 75
West Coast 8, 48-51, 68, 69
Western Springs 18
Westhaven Marina 14
Westland National Park 49, 50, 51, 69
Westport 48, 49, 69
Whakapapa 36, 37
Whakarewarewa 33, 34
Whakatane 26, 27
Whangaehu River 33, 37
Whangamata 20, 21
Whanganui National Park 40
Whanganui River 38 40-41
Whangarei 10, 12,
Whitcombe Pass 68
White Island 26, 27
Whitianga 20
Wilding, Anthony 67
Wilding Park 67
World Heritage Area 49, 52, 69

Sources of further information

There are many helpful references for those who want to learn more about New Zealand. Here's a select few that I have been particularly impressed with. Many more can be found in bookshops and local libraries.

Useful books:
Bateman New Zealand Encyclopedia, David Bateman, Auckland 1992.
Kirkpatrick, Russell, *Bateman Contemporary Atlas New Zealand*, David Bateman, Auckland 1999.
Macmillan New Zealand World Atlas, Macmillan, Auckland 1999.
McKinnon, Malcolm (editor), *Bateman New Zealand Historical Atlas*, David Bateman, Auckland 1997.
Pope, Diana and Jeremy, *Mobil New Zealand Travel Guide, North Island*, Reed, Auckland 1996.
Pope, Diana and Jeremy, *Mobil New Zealand Travel Guide, South Island*, Reed, Auckland 1995.
Reed, A.W., *Place Names of New Zealand*, A.H. & A.W. Reed, Wellington 1975.
Statistics New Zealand, *New Zealand Official Yearbook 1998*, GP Publications, Wellington 1998.

Recommended magazines:
Forest & Bird, Royal Forest and Bird Protection Society of New Zealand, Wellington.
New Zealand Geographic, New Zealand Geographic Publications Ltd, Auckland.

Helpful websites:
www.arc.govt.nz — Auckland Regional Council has the city's volcanoes on-line.
www.forest-bird.org.nz — NZ Forest and Bird Society keeps you up to date with conservation issues and campaigns.
www.gns.cri.nz — Institute of Geological and Nuclear Sciences lets you log on to the latest earthquake!
www.purenz.com — New Zealand Tourism lets you see what's on offer throughout the country.
www.stats.govt.nz — Statistics New Zealand has those statistical details you're looking for.

Organisations:
Various organisations are excellent sources of local information. These include the following:
Automobile Association: Members are entitled to free maps for all regions. The maps are backed with detailed natural, historical and geographical information. Non-members can buy from an excellent range of informative publications.
Department of Conservation: Contact local conservancy offices or visitor centres.
Visitor Information Network: Contact local visitor information offices.